# Haydn R
# Junior English 1
# *Revised Edition*

Revised by Angela Burt
Adviser: Patricia Lewis

**Acknowledgements**

Grateful acknowledgement is made to the following for permission to use copyright material:

page 36 **Knock down the tower**
*Science in the Kitchen* (page 8) by Rebecca Heddle.
By kind permission of the publishers Usborne Publishing Ltd.

45 **The Vulture**
By Hilaire Belloc from *Cautionary Verses*.
By kind permission of the publishers G Duckworth & Co Ltd.

54 **Caterpillar**
By kind permission of Wendy Cope.

90 **The summer holiday**
*The Ghost Child* by Emma Tennant.
Published by Grafton Books.

Every effort has been made to obtain permission for copyright materials. The publishers would be grateful for any discrepancies to be notified.

Designed by Michael Soderberg
Illustrated by Barry Rowe, Martin White, David Atkinson, Vali Herzer and Hardlines.

© Haydn Richards 1965
Revised edition 1997

ARP impression 98

ISBN 978 0 602 27508 2 (without answers)
ISBN 978 0 602 27509 9 (with answers)

Ginn is an imprint of Pearson Education Limited, a company incorporated in England and Wales, having its registered office at Edinburgh Gate, Harlow, Essex, CM20 2JE.
Registered company number: 872828
Ginn on the internet http://www.ginn.co.uk

Filmset by Wyvern Typesetting Ltd, Bristol
Printed in the United Kingdom by
Ashford Colour Press Ltd, Gosport, Hants.

# Preface to the Revised Edition

This revised and updated edition of Haydn Richards' popular series meets the appropriate requirements of the 1995 National Curriculum for English at Key Stage 1 and Key Stage 2. It is also in line with the requirements of the Northern Ireland and Scottish 5-14 curricula.

Particular care has been taken while incorporating changes to preserve the successful format, tone and clarity of the original series.

Those already familiar with Junior English will see that in this revised edition there is now increased coverage of spelling, punctuation and grammar topics in each of the four books and that formal grammatical terminology, in response to popular request, is now used from the very beginning. Throughout the series, both the range and complexity of the reading comprehension exercises have been extended. Additional vocabulary exercises have been introduced together with a number of dictionary practice exercises to encourage the early use of dictionaries and thesauruses.

The series, as well as preparing pupils for National Curriculum assessment, also provides a sound basis for those preparing for 11+ English entrance examinations to independent schools. The current ISEB 11+ English syllabus was taken into account during the revision of Junior English.

Angela Burt

# Contents

| | | |
|---|---|---|
| Abbreviations | | |
| *Mr. Mrs. Dr.* | 15 | |
| Addresses | 22 | |
| Adjectives | 64 75 80 86 89 | |
| Alphabetical order | 10 32 | |
| Apostrophe | | |
| *Contractions* | 51 | |
| *Possession* | 61 | |
| Capital letters | | |
| *Beginning sentence* | 11 | |
| *Days of week* | 20 | |
| *I* | 14 | |
| *Initials* | 15 | |
| *Names of persons* | 15 | |
| *Place names* | 22 | |
| *Various* | 11 14 53 | |
| Collective nouns | 59 | |
| Colours | 26 | |
| Commas | 73 | |
| Compounds | 55 | |
| Comprehension | 6 12 18 24 30 36 42 48 54 60 | |
| | 66 72 78 84 90 | |
| Contractions | | |
| *The* not *words* | 51 | |
| Days of the week | 20 | |
| Dictionary practice | 26 63 74 82 | |
| Gender | 19 | |
| Group names | 62 | |
| Homes of creatures | 74 89 | |
| Homophones | 49 58 65 89 | |
| Initials | 15 | |

| | | | | | |
|---:|---|---|---|---|---|
| Nouns | 1 | 2 | 3 | | |
| Numbers | | | | | |
| *1 to 19* | 4 | 25 | | | |
| *Over 19* | 25 | | | | |
| Occupations | 50 | | | | |
| Opposites | | | | | |
| *Prefix* un | 37 | | | | |
| *Change of word* | 38 | 57 | 89 | | |
| Plurals | | | | | |
| *Adding -s* | 17 | | | | |
| *Adding -es* | 21 | | | | |
| *Changing* y *to* i | 27 | | | | |
| *Changing* f *to* v | 28 | | | | |
| *Various* | 89 | | | | |
| Poems | 45 | 54 | 68 | | |
| Prepositions | 40 | | | | |
| Pronouns | 88 | | | | |
| Punctuation | | | | | |
| *Full stop* | 8 | | | | |
| *Question mark* | 9 | | | | |
| Revision | 89 | | | | |
| Rhymes | 16 | 45 | 68 | 79 | |
| Sentences | | | | | |
| *Arranging in order* | 70 | | | | |
| *Beginning* | 46 | 69 | 81 | | |
| *Ending* | 73 | 81 | 87 | | |
| *Composing* | 7 | 8 | 9 | 11 | 73 | 75 |
| *Jumbled* | 35 | | | | |
| *Joining with conjunctions* | 43 | 67 | 71 | 87 | |
| *Using* and | 43 | | | | |
| *Using* but | 67 | | | | |
| *Using* because | 71 | | | | |
| *Using* before | 87 | | | | |
| *Matching parts* | 77 | | | | |
| Similars | 63 | 82 | 89 | | |

| | | |
|---|---|---|
| Similes | 85 | |
| Things we eat and drink | 44 | |
| Usage | | |
| *a, an* | 3 | |
| *did, done* | 69 | |
| *do, does* | 52 | |
| *has, have* | 46 | |
| *is, are* | 31 | |
| *saw, seen* | 77 | |
| *to, too, two* | 23 | |
| *was, were* | 31 | |
| Verbs | 5  7  13  29  33  34  39  56 | |
| Verbal intelligence | 76  83 | |
| Words with more than one meaning | 47 | |

# The game of I spy

**A** Do you know the game of **I Spy**?
Look at the first picture.
I spy with my little eye
Something beginning with **c**.

1  c _ _

This is a **cup**, so you write the word **cup**.
Now do the same with the other pictures.

2  p _ _        3  b _ _ _      4  s _ _ _

5  d _ _        6  l _ _        7  t _ _ _

8  f _ _ _      9  j _ _        10  e _ _

**B** Which word fills the gap?

1  A hen laid the ____ .

2  The ____ can bark.

3  A ____ lives in water.

4  A ____ is worn on the foot.

1

# Nouns

bag  drum
bed  lamp
book  pen
clock  spoon
door  tap

**A** Write in order, 1 to 10, the names of the things in the pictures. Look at the list of words on the left.

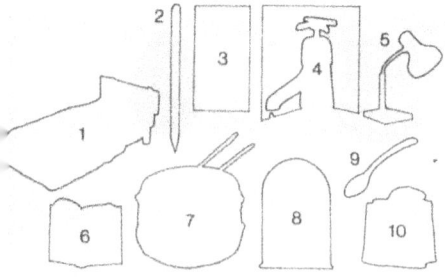

The words you have written are the **names** of things. We call such words **nouns**.

**B** What am I?

1 You beat me with two sticks.
2 You lie on me when you go to sleep.
3 I can give light when it is dark.
4 You open me when you enter a room.
5 You carry all your shopping in me.
6 You look at me when you read.
7 You come to me for water.
8 People use me to stir their tea.
9 You may use me when you write.
10 I tell you the time.

# Using a and an

apple    envelope
arrow    iron
axe    onion
eggcup    oven

**A** Write the names of these things, putting **an** in front of each. The words you need are in the list on the left.

Always write **an** before words beginning with

**a  e  i  o  u**

Always write **a** before words beginning with other letters.

**B** Write **a** or **an** before each of these words.

1 \_\_\_\_ clock
2 \_\_\_\_ armchair
3 \_\_\_\_ orchard
4 \_\_\_\_ book
5 \_\_\_\_ pen
6 \_\_\_\_ arch
7 \_\_\_\_ tree
8 \_\_\_\_ door
9 \_\_\_\_ elephant
10 \_\_\_\_ ostrich
11 \_\_\_\_ eagle
12 \_\_\_\_ hoop
13 \_\_\_\_ desk
14 \_\_\_\_ island
15 \_\_\_\_ umbrella

# Numbers

**1**
**one**

**2**
**two**

**3**
**three**

**4**
**four**

**5**
**five**

**6**
**six**

**7**
**seven**

**8**
**eight**

**9**
**nine**

**10**
**ten**

**A** Fill each space with the right word.

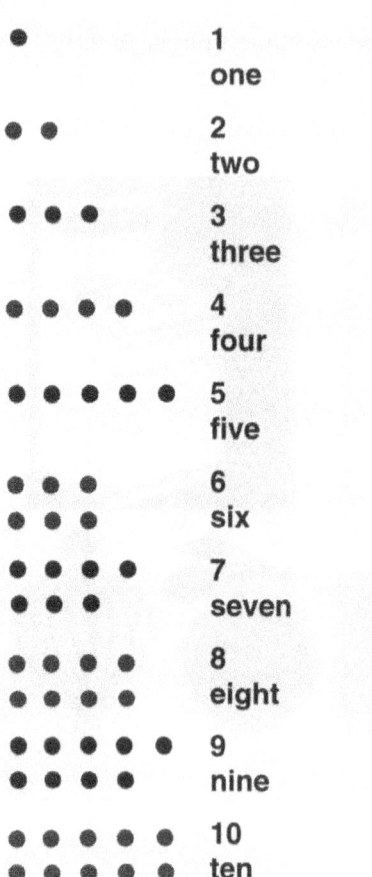

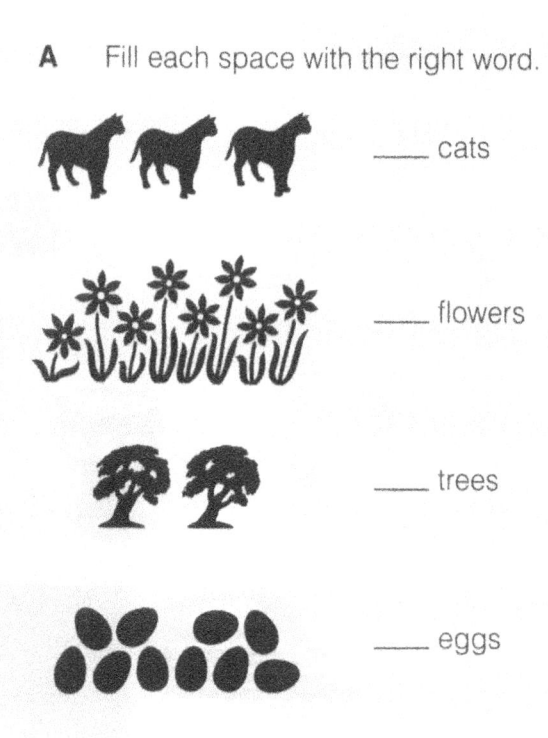

____ cats

____ flowers

____ trees

____ eggs

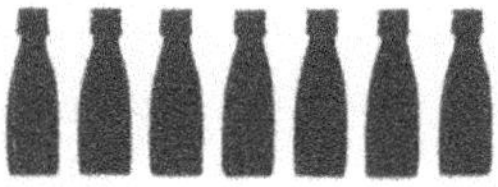

____ bottles

**11** one and ten = **eleven**

**12** two and ten = **twelve** (dozen)

**13** three and ten = **thirteen**

**14** four and ten = **fourteen**

**15** five and ten = **fifteen**

**16** six and ten = **sixteen**

**17** seven and ten = **seventeen**

**18** eight and ten = **eighteen**

**19** nine and ten = **nineteen**

**B**

1 Which word means three and ten?

2 Write the word for 19.

3 ____ is one less than twelve.

4 William is fourteen years old. He will be ____ next birthday.

5 Write the words for the four even numbers between eleven and nineteen.

# Verbs

Verbs are **doing** words.

eating      jumping
drinking    reading
fishing     sleeping
flying      washing

Look at the pictures.

**A**  Write the word which fills each gap.

1  The man is ____ his car.
2  The boy is ____ under the tree.
3  The two boys are ____ .
4  The girl is ____ an apple.
5  The woman is ____ a book.
6  The dog is ____ over a log.
7  The birds are ____ high.
8  The cat is ____ milk.

**B**  Add **-ing** to each of these words.

1  call      5  pull     9   sing
2  draw      6  see      10  bark
3  do        7  hear     11  teach
4  try       8  rain     12  feel

# Pam's pet

Pam's pet is a cat named Punch. Punch has a coat of soft black fur. Pam gives him milk every day. He laps it up with his long pink tongue. Then he purrs to show that he is happy.

He often sits on the rug by the fire. There he washes his face with his soft paws. His claws are very sharp, but he does not scratch Pam. Punch keeps mice away from the house.

Copy the sentences.
Fill each space with the right word.

1  Pam's cat is ____ in colour.

2  When Punch is happy, he ____ .

3  He uses his ____ to drink the milk.

4  Punch likes sitting by the ____ .

5  He washes his face with his ____ .

6  His paws are ____ .

7  His claws are ____ .

8  Punch keeps ____ away from the house.

# More verbs

**A** Look at the pictures.
Make a list of the verbs. Number them from 1 to 8.

When **-ing** is added to a verb ending with **e**, the **e** is dropped.

**B** Use the words in the list on the left to fill these gaps.

| | |
|---|---|
| dance | dancing |
| dive | diving |
| drive | driving |
| hide | hiding |
| ride | riding |
| skate | skating |
| wave | waving |
| write | writing |

1 Sam likes ____ his new pony.
2 Ben was ____ in the bushes.
3 We saw Zoë ____ to us across the road.
4 Soraya uses pen and ink when she is ____ .
5 Stephen passed his ____ test first time.
6 Michael loved ____ off the high board.
7 Kate takes tap ____ lessons every Tuesday.
8 People were ____ on the frozen pond.

7

# Statements

Read this sentence.

**A cat has sharp claws.**

This sentence tells us something about a cat.

It is called a **statement**.

Every statement must end with a **full stop**.

**A** Copy these statements and put a full stop at the end of each.

1. Butter is made from milk
2. Honey is made by bees
3. Sugar has a sweet taste
4. The school bus was late today
5. Mary had dinner at school
6. I put some coal on the fire
7. We go blackberrying in the autumn
8. The crocus is a spring flower
9. The elephant has a long trunk
10. A young cat is called a kitten

**B** Now write one statement about each of these things.

1. a cow
2. your home
3. any tree
4. yourself
5. your toys
6. any bird

# Questions

Some sentences ask a question.

What is your name?

How old are you?

Where do you live?

Every **question** must end with a **question mark**.

**A** Copy these questions and put a question mark at the end of each.

1 How are you today
2 Why were you late this morning
3 Where did you put the sweets
4 When are you coming to see me
5 Who told you that I was ill
6 Which of these toys do you like best
7 Will you come swimming with me
8 Did you remember to post the letter
9 Have you seen John
10 Can you tell me the way

**B** Now write one question about each of these things.

1 the time       4 a farm
2 the weather    5 money
3 a book         6 clothes

# The alphabet

This is the alphabet written in lower case (small) letters.

a b c d e f g h i j k l m
n o p q r s t u v w x y z

You should learn the alphabet well.

From these twenty-six letters all our words are made.

**A**

1  What is the fifth letter?
2  Write the last letter of all.
3  Which letter comes next after **s**?
4  Which letter comes just before **h**?
5  Write the letter which comes between **k** and **m**.
6  Write the two letters on either side of **e**.
7  Which letter is next but one after **q**?
8  Which letter is next but one before **j**?
9  What are the missing letters?
   m  n     p  q  r     t  u     w  x
10 What word do the missing letters spell?
   a     c  d     f     h

These letters are jumbled up:
c  e  a  d  b

Now they are in the right
**a b c** order:
a  b  c  d  e

**B**  Place the letters below in **a b c** order.

1  n  p  o  l  m
2  v  y  w  u  x
3  q  r  u  t  v  s
4  d  f  b  a  e  c
5  i  k  h  g  f  j

10

# Capital letters beginning a sentence

Every sentence, both statements and questions, must begin with a **capital letter** (upper case).

**Small** (lower case) letters    a b c d e f g h i j
**Capital** (upper case) letters    A B C D E F G H I J

**A**    Copy these sentences.
Begin each with a capital letter.

Put a **full stop** at the end of each **statement**.

Put a **question mark** at the end of each **question**.

1. honey is sweet
2. the sun sets in the west
3. do you like nuts
4. a rabbit has soft fur
5. when will you be ready
6. keep off the grass
7. this meat is very tender
8. are you going shopping
9. look where you are going
10. what is the right time

**B**    Write six sentences about the rabbit.
Say something about –

1. its fur
2. its ears
3. its tail
4. its teeth
5. its whiskers
6. its home

# The Hall family

ball
banana
book
cat
family
fire
five
floor
girl
hands
letter
mother
television

Use the words in the list on the left to fill the gaps in these sentences.

1   This is the Hall ____ .
2   There are ____ people in all.
3   The father is reading a ____ .
4   He is also eating a ____ .
5   The ____ is writing a ____ .
6   The baby is sitting on the ____ .
7   He has a ____ in his ____ .
8   The ____ is playing with the ____ .
9   The dog is asleep by the ____ .
10  The boy is watching the ____ .

# Verbs

When we add **-ing** to some verbs we **double the last letter**.

| | |
|---|---|
| bat | batting |
| chop | chopping |
| clap | clapping |
| cut | cutting |
| run | running |
| sit | sitting |
| skip | skipping |
| swim | swimming |

**A** Make a list of the verbs which fit these pictures. Number them from 1 to 8, according to the plan at the bottom of the page.

**B** Fill the gap in each sentence by adding **-ing** to the word in bold type at the end of each line.

1. Sam kept ____ on the ice. **slip**
2. Anna enjoyed ____ the garden. **dig**
3. The bus will be ____ at the school gates. **stop**
4. We shall be ____ off there. **get**
5. The leaves lay ____ on the ground. **rot**
6. I am ____ my toys away. **put**
7. Mina went out without ____ the door. **shut**
8. Megan was ____ a new sweater. **knit**

# Capital letters

This girl's name is Sumitra Patel.

The name of her pet cat is Mina.

The girl's last name, **Patel**, is her **surname**.

Her other name, **Sumitra**, is her **first name**.

The names of people and pets always begin with a **capital letter**.

**A** Write your first name and your surname.

Now write out these sentences, using capital letters for the names of people and pets.

1 I told mary that I would play with her after tea.
2 When emma fell down lee helped her up.
3 I think david maggs is taller than john perry.
4 The names of the twins are bela and ramu.
5 I saw sean baker feeding his dog sam.
6 We saw daisy the cow being milked.
7 kayleigh named her new pony sunshine.
8 The name of our cat is sooty.

The word **I** is always a capital letter.

What shall **I** have to eat?

**B** Write a capital **I** in each space.

1 Where did ___ put my comb?
2 Do you think ___ am tall for my age?
3 Becky said ___ could have an orange.
4 ___ think ___ have a cold coming on.
5 When ___ am tired ___ lie down and rest.

14

# Names and initials

Mr. Brown        Mrs. Brown

Miss James

Dr. Costello

The name of Joan's father is Mr. Norman Brown.

Her mother's name is Mrs. June Brown.

The name of Joan's teacher is Miss Freda James.

The family doctor is Dr. John Costello.

Instead of writing a person's first name, we sometimes write only the first letter.

For **Richard** we write **R**.

For **Mary** we write **M**.

We call these letters **initials**.

**Initials** are always followed by a **full stop**.

**Mr.** is a short way of writing **Mister**.

**Mrs.** is a short way of writing **Mistress**.

There is no short way of writing **Miss**.

**Dr.** is a short way of writing **Doctor**.

Write these names the short way, using initials for the first names.

**A**
1. Mister John Cobb
2. Mister Harjit Singh
3. Mister David Roy Bond

**B**
1. Mistress Irene Bevan
2. Mistress Kamal Robinson
3. Mistress Joy Ann Davis

**C**
1. Miss Jennifer Mason
2. Miss Wai Leung
3. Miss Anna May Carr

**D**
1. Doctor Pedro Soto
2. Doctor Anna Jane Browne
3. Doctor Mark Ian Fox

# Rhymes

Pussy Cat, Pussy Cat, where have you been?
I've been to London to look at the Queen.
Pussy Cat, Pussy Cat, what did you there?
I frightened a little mouse under the chair.

The words **been** and **Queen** end with the same sound.

Words which end with the same sound are said to **rhyme.**

**A** Write the two words that rhyme in each group below.

| 1 | man | 2 | bed | 3 | same |
|---|---|---|---|---|---|
|   | far |   | bee |   | take |
|   | bat |   | leg |   | tail |
|   | can |   | pen |   | pane |
|   | tap |   | pet |   | sail |
|   | wag |   | see |   | race |

| 4 | team | 5 | fear | 6 | train |
|---|---|---|---|---|---|
|   | seat |   | beat |   | laid |
|   | lean |   | bear |   | wait |
|   | leap |   | hail |   | pain |
|   | seed |   | pear |   | sail |
|   | meat |   | real |   | page |

**B** Here are twenty words. Write them as ten pairs of words which rhyme, like this:

trip     sore     mill
ship     more     fill

1  trip      8   trees     15  feel
2  sore      9   pull      16  card
3  mill     10   hard      17  full
4  down     11   brown     18  fill
5  line     12   fine      19  bees
6  peel     13   ship      20  harm
7  more     14   farm

# Plurals

one chick    two chicks

one bear    three bears

**A** Write the missing words.

four ___    five ___    two ___

three ___    six ___    seven___

**B** Copy these nouns.
Write **s** after each to make it mean **more than one**.

1  hen      5  duck     9   nut
2  cow      6  horse    10  sweet
3  ship     7  boat     11  cap
4  pen      8  sock     12  shoe

**C** Copy these sentences.
Fill each space by adding **-s** to the word in bold type.

1  Clare gave her mother a box of ___ . **chocolate**

2  Simon has two ___ . **sister**

3  You can have five ___ . **sweet**

4  Cats have very sharp ___ . **claw**

5  Ian has read ten ___ this week. **comic**

6  Who will help me blow up these ___ ? **balloon**

7  Do you like pop-up ___ ? **book**

17

# Busy children

boys
easel
five
front
girls
house
jar

looking
painting
pencils
picture
rabbit
showing
table

Look at the picture carefully.
Use the names below and the words in the list on the left to fill the gaps.

1   There are ____ children in the picture.
2   Two of them are ____ and three are ____ .
3   James has made a ____ out of clay.
4   Louise has done a drawing and is ____ it to ____ .
5   There is a ____ of water in ____ of Ian.
6   Megan is ____ a ____ of a house.
7   Her picture is standing on the ____ .
8   Ann has a set of coloured ____ .
9   ____ and ____ are sitting opposite each other.
10  ____ is the only child standing.

Ian          Louise          James          Megan          Ann

18

# He and she

A **boy** is a **he**.

A **girl** is a **she**.

| **He** | **She** |
|---|---|
| boy | girl |
| brother | sister |
| father | mother |
| husband | wife |
| king | queen |
| lord | lady |
| man | woman |
| nephew | niece |
| prince | princess |
| uncle | aunt |

**A**  Learn the words in the list on the left, then write the words which are missing from each sentence.

1  His mother and ____ are both very tall.
2  James spent a holiday with his uncle and ____ .
3  There is work to do for every man and ____ .
4  Tony took his ____ and niece to the museum.
5  Both husband and ____ played tennis badly.
6  The king and ____ ruled for many years.
7  Tom and Emma are brother and ____ .
8  Tom is a lazy boy. Emma is a grumpy ____ .

**B**  Give the missing words.

1  ____ and wife
2  ____ and lady
3  ____ and aunt
4  ____ and niece
5  ____ and sister
6  ____ and princess
7  ____ and mother
8  ____ and queen

# Days of the week

1 Sunday
2 Monday
3 Tuesday
4 Wednesday
5 Thursday
6 Friday
7 Saturday

The name of every day of the week begins with a **capital letter**.

Learn the names of the days and the order in which they come.

**Solomon Grundy**

Solomon Grundy,
Born on a Monday,
Christened on Tuesday,
Married on Wednesday,
Took ill on Thursday,
Worse on Friday,
Died on Saturday,
Buried on Sunday
That was the end of
Solomon Grundy.

Write the name of the day which will fill each gap in these sentences.

1 If today is Wednesday, yesterday was ____ .
2 Which day of the week has most letters in its name?
3 ____ comes between Wednesday and Friday.
4 The day before Thursday is ____ .
5 Solomon Grundy was born on a ____ .
6 On ____ many people go to church.
7 If today is Friday, then tomorrow will be ____ .
8 Which day has in its name the letter **d** which is silent?
9 Sunday is the first day of the week. Which is the last day?
10 If you place the days of the week in **a b c** order, which day comes first?

# Plurals

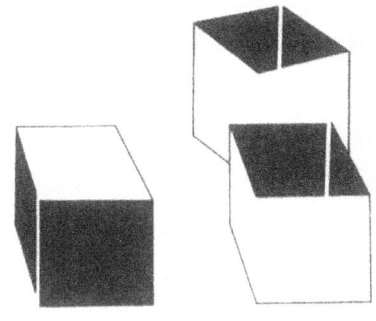

one box      two box**es**

We add **-es** to box to show **more than one**.

one bus      three bus**es**

We add **-es** to bus to show **more than one**.

**A** Write the missing words. Each ends with **-es**.

1. one bush     four _____
2. one watch     six _____
3. one coach     two _____
4. one brush     five _____
5. one box     nine _____
6. one peach     a dish of _____
7. a dish     a set of _____
8. a church     a few _____
9. a torch     many _____
10. a match     a box of _____

**B** Use the words you have made to fill these gaps.

1. The jeweller sold many different clocks and _____ .
2. There were lots of gooseberries on the _____ .
3. Many _____ have a tall tower.
4. Janet dropped the _____ on the floor.
5. The man used four _____ to light the fire.
6. Two _____ took the party to town.
7. Joseph got the _____ to clean his shoes.
8. Emma was given two _____ of chocolates.
9. Adrian bought a tin of _____ and a pot of cream.
10. Some _____ throw their light a long way.

# Capital letters

Look at this address.

The **name of the street** begins with a **capital letter**.

The **name of the town** begins with a **capital letter**.

The **name of the county**, Sussex, and the postcode have **capital letters**.

The names of places always begin with a **capital letter**.

>  Miss Ann Page,
>  24 Main Street,
>  Brighton,
>  Sussex,
>  BR1 3HS

**A** Write these sentences, using capital letters for the names of all places. End each sentence with a full stop.

1. london is the capital of england
2. Ships sail from dover
3. He was born in oxford
4. bath is a very old city
5. Jane lives in ashton road, bristol
6. We went by train to york
7. The aeroplane landed at heathrow
8. The biggest city in wales is cardiff
9. Many people visit windsor castle
10. He has moved from station road to oak avenue

**B**

1. Write your own name and address.
2. Write the name and address of any friend.
3. Write the name and address of any relation.

# To, two and too

**To**, **two** and **too** all have a similar sound.

Going **to** bed

Going **to** sleep

The **two** dogs

Each has **two** ears

He is **too** old to work. (more than enough)

He is very bent, **too**.

**To**, **two** and **too** have different meanings.

Write **to**, **two** or **too** in each space below.

1 Alan went ___ bed early.

2 ___ and ___ make four.

3 He is ___ ill ___ go ___ school.

4 It is nearly ___ o'clock.

5 Are you going ___ help me?

6 I am going ___ sit down in the shade.

7 It is ___ hot ___ play games.

8 The ___ girls were great friends.

9 Are you coming ___ London, ___?

10 Jason is ___ young ___ drive.

# Children at play

Look at these children at play. Use the words from the list on the left to finish each sentence below.

branch
fast
holding
marbles
ring
skates
skipping
stick
swing
thick

1  David is on roller ____ .
2  He is going very ____ .
3  Pavana and Ann are having a ____ race.
4  Chandra and James are playing ____ .
5  James is ____ a marble in his right hand.
6  Jane is on the ____ .
7  The swing hangs from a ____ of the tree.
8  The trunk of the tree is very ____ .

# Numbers

20 **twenty** means **two tens**
30 **thirty** means **three tens**
40 **forty** means **four tens**
50 **fifty** means **five tens**
60 **sixty** means **six tens**
70 **seventy** means **seven tens**
80 **eighty** means **eight tens**
90 **ninety** means **nine tens**
100 **one hundred** means **ten tens**

**A** Write the words which fill the gaps.

1 Seven tens are ____ .
2 The number ____ is one half of one hundred.
3 Four times ten are ____ .
4 Six rows of ten make ____ .
5 Three tens are ____ .

When we write a **units** word after a **tens** word we use a hyphen -.

65 sixty-five
29 twenty-nine
36 thirty-six

**B** Write the words for –

a 42
b 97
c 78
d 54
e 83

**C** Remember all you have learned about spelling numbers on this page and on page 4 and write the words for these numbers.

a 14         f 5
b 8          g 21
c 99         h 11
d 13         i 86
e 30         j 100

# Colours

Look at the list of colours below.

Learn how to spell each word, then answer the questions.

black
blue
brown
green
grey
red
white
yellow

**A** What are the colours of these things?

1. a buttercup
2. grass
3. tar
4. blood
5. chocolate
6. a postbox
7. a ripe banana
8. a snowdrop
9. a ripe tomato
10. a polar bear

**B** Write these sentences, putting in the missing words.

1. In spring the leaves on the trees are ____ .
2. When the traffic light is ____ the traffic must stop.
3. When the traffic light is ____ the traffic can go.
4. Butter is ____ in colour.
5. The roofs of the houses were ____ with snow.
6. On a cloudless day the sky is ____ .
7. A lump of coal is ____ in colour.
8. When bread is toasted it turns ____ .
9. The robin has a ____ breast.
10. When people get old their hair turns ____ or ____ .

**C** Use your dictionary to help you find out the colours of these jewels used to make rings, bracelets and necklaces.

1. emerald
2. sapphire
3. ruby
4. pearl

26

# Plurals

one pon**y**    two pon**ies**

one dais**y**    four dais**ies**

To make the words **pony** and **daisy plural** (mean **more than one**) we change the **y** to **i** before adding **-es**.

| pony | daisy |
|---|---|
| poni | daisi |
| ponies | daisies |

**A** Now do the same with these words which end with **y**.

1  fly       a swarm of _____
2  pony      two _____
3  puppy     a litter of _____
4  berry     a cluster of _____
5  daisy     a chain of _____
6  spy       several _____
7  story     a book of _____
8  fairy     many _____
9  baby      four _____
10 lady      a few _____

**B** Use the words you have made to fill these gaps.

1  Holly _____ are red when they are ripe.
2  Young _____ are fed on milk.
3  Our corgi had four _____ today.
4  Three _____ were grazing in the field.
5  David likes to read _____ about animals.
6  The _____ used hidden cameras.
7  Several _____ were buzzing around the jam.
8  Do you believe in _____?

**C** Make these words plural.

1  city       4  hobby
2  party      5  butterfly
3  lorry

# More plurals

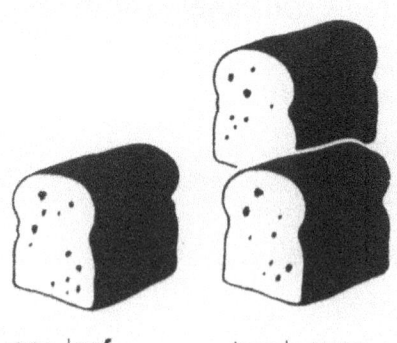

one loaf     two loa**ves**

one leaf     three lea**ves**

To make the words **loaf** and **leaf plural** (mean **more than one**) we change the **f** to **v** before adding **-es**.

loaf     leaf
loav     leav
loaves     leaves

**A**    Now do the same with these words.

1   thief        ten \_\_\_\_
2   shelf       three \_\_\_\_
3   loaf         five \_\_\_\_
4   half         two \_\_\_\_
5   calf         four \_\_\_\_
6   leaf         many \_\_\_\_
7   sheaf       ten \_\_\_\_
8   wolf        a pack of \_\_\_\_

With these words, change the **f** to **v** and add **-s**. The **e** is there already.

9    wife \_\_\_\_
10   life \_\_\_\_
11   knife \_\_\_\_

**B**    Use the words you have made to fill these gaps.

1   The \_\_\_\_ in the shop were full of toys.
2   The baker sold dozens of \_\_\_\_ of bread yesterday.
3   In autumn \_\_\_\_ fall from many trees.
4   There are two \_\_\_\_ in a whole one.
5   Baby cows are called \_\_\_\_ .
6   \_\_\_\_ hunt in packs.
7   The butcher has very sharp \_\_\_\_ .
8   The police caught the car \_\_\_\_ .

# Adding -ed to verbs

To make a verb show **past time** we add **-ed**.

| Now | Past |
|---|---|
| Today I play. | Yesterday I play**ed**. |
| Today I work. | Last week I work**ed**. |

**A** Add **-ed** to each of these verbs.

1  rain
2  play
3  chew
4  wait
5  ask
6  bark
7  fill
8  pick
9  open
10  fetch

**B** Use the words you have made to fill the gaps in these sentences.

1  Jane ____ her mother for another cake.
2  Simon ____ an apple off the tree.
3  The dog ____ at the postman.
4  Jill ____ the paper for her parents.
5  The kitten ____ with the ball.
6  The man ____ for an hour for the bus.
7  Terry ____ the bucket with water.
8  It ____ all day yesterday.
9  The cow ____ the grass for a long time.
10  He ____ the door and went in.

# Martin's toys

Martin has a big cupboard full of toys. Some are new but most of them are old. He will not get rid of any of them.

The toy he likes best is his clockwork train. The oldest toy is a teddy bear. His mother bought it for his first birthday.

Martin also has a big crane and a tractor. These are almost new. The crane can lift the tractor right off the floor.

1  Where does Martin keep his toys?

2  Which toy does Martin like best?

3  Who bought the teddy bear for Martin?

4  Which toy does Martin lift off the floor with his crane?

5  Is it true that most of Martin's toys are new?

# Using is and are/Using was and were

The tree **is** bare.
We use **is** for **one** tree.

The trees **are** bare.
We use **are** for **more than one**.

We use **was** for one person or thing.

We use **were** for more than one person or thing.

**A** Fill each space with **is** or **are**.

1 This apple ___ sour.
  These apples ___ sour.

2 ___ the house old?
  ___ the houses old?

3 The dog ___ barking.
  The dogs ___ barking.

4 ___ the egg fresh?
  ___ the eggs fresh?

**B** Fill each space with **was** or **were**.

1 One egg ___ cracked.
  Three eggs ___ cracked.

2 The girl ___ skipping.
  The girls ___ skipping.

3 ___ the orange sweet?
  ___ the oranges sweet?

4 The cow ___ being milked.
  The cows ___ being milked.

**C** Choose the right word from the pair above to fill each space.

1 **is    are**
  Barbara ___ ill, but Anna ___ well.

2 **was    were**
  The hens ___ laying, so the farmer ___ pleased.

3 **was    were**
  The wind ___ cold and snow ___ falling.

4 **is    are**
  School ___ over and we ___ going home.

5 **was    were**
  They ___ glad because the day ___ sunny.

31

# The alphabet

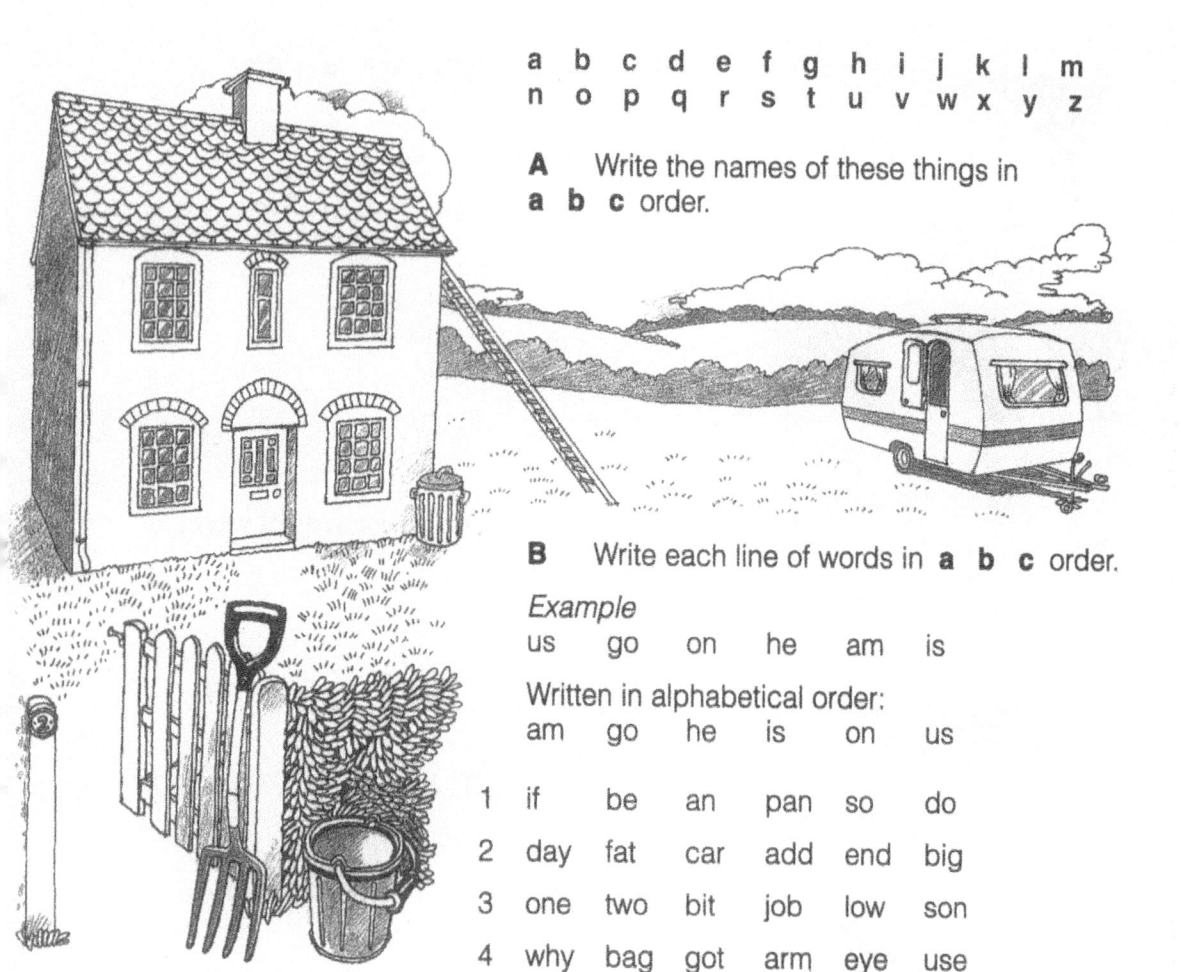

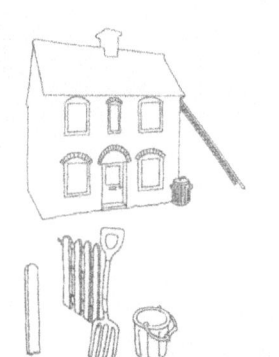

a b c d e f g h i j k l m
n o p q r s t u v w x y z

**A** Write the names of these things in **a b c** order.

**B** Write each line of words in **a b c** order.

*Example*
us   go   on   he   am   is

Written in alphabetical order:
am   go   he   is   on   us

1  if    be   an   pan  so   do
2  day   fat  car  add  end  big
3  one   two  bit  job  low  son
4  why   bag  got  arm  eye  use

**C** In each group below all the words are in **a b c** order except one. Can you spot the odd word?

In group 1 below the odd word is **gun**.

| 1 | arm | 2 | hat | 3 | bed | 4 | fat | 5 | queen |
|---|ball|   | zoo |   | ear |   | goat|   | ring |
|   | can |   | jar |   | kid |   | hut |   | bell |
|   | deer|   | log |   | net |   | wet |   | tray |
|   | **gun** | | man |   | pad |   | ink |   | use |
|   | egg |   | peg |   | cow |   | jug |   | van |
|   | fan |   | rat |   | sun |   | king|   | web |

# Verbs past time

To make a verb show **past time** we add **-ed**.

|  Now | Past |
|---|---|
| Today I play. | Yesterday I play**ed**. |
| Today I work. | Last week I work**ed**. |

But if the verb ends with **e** we just add **-d**.

The snails move slowly.   The snails move**d** slowly.

**A** Make each of these verbs show **past time** by adding **-d**.

1 sneeze    5 hope    9 save
2 like      6 wave    10 joke
3 wipe      7 use     11 bake
4 fire      8 dive    12 move

**B** Make the word to fill each space by adding **-d** or **-ed** to the word in bold type.

1 William ___ loudly.    **cough**
2 They ___ last Monday.    **arrive**
3 The crowd ___ the Queen.    **cheer**
4 Helen ___ sausages for us.    **cook**
5 We ___ for you.    **wait**
6 Sam ___ to school.    **cycle**
7 Dad ___ his present.    **love**
8 Everyone ___ very happy.    **look**
9 Camilla ___ her teeth.    **clean**
10 Sue ___ very carefully.    **watch**

33

# Adding -ed to verbs

When we add **-ed** to some verbs we **double the last letter**.

|  | rob | tug |
|---|---|---|
| Double the last letter | rob**b** | tug**g** |
| Add on **-ed** | rob**bed** | tug**ged** |

**A**  Add **-ed** to each of these verbs. Remember to double the last letter.

1  pin
2  clap
3  stop
4  slip
5  tap
6  hug
7  wag
8  chop
9  hum
10  sip

**B**  Use the words you have made to fill the gaps in these sentences.

1  The little boy ____ on the ice.
2  The dog ____ his tail.
3  James ____ the hot tea slowly.
4  The bus ____ outside the school.
5  Jane ____ her new teddy bear.
6  Alan ____ on the door before going in.
7  Carol ____ a badge on to her jacket.
8  The scouts ____ the wood for the fire.
9  The children ____ their hands for joy.
10  A swarm of bees ____ around our heads.

# Jumbled sentences

The words in this sentence are not in their right order.

a has tail monkey The long

This sentence has the words in their right order.

The monkey has a long tail.

Put the words in these sentences in their correct order.

The capital letter shows which word comes first.

Put a full stop at the end of each sentence.

1. sheep We from wool the get

2. climbing girl is a tree The

3. grass is The cow some eating

4. very donkey A ears long has

5. a horse is cart The pulling

6. is boy a The bicycle riding

35

# Knock down the tower

Make a tower of four sugar lumps on a plate. Add a little food colouring to some water. Pour it on to the plate and watch what happens.

**Watch the bottom of the tower.**

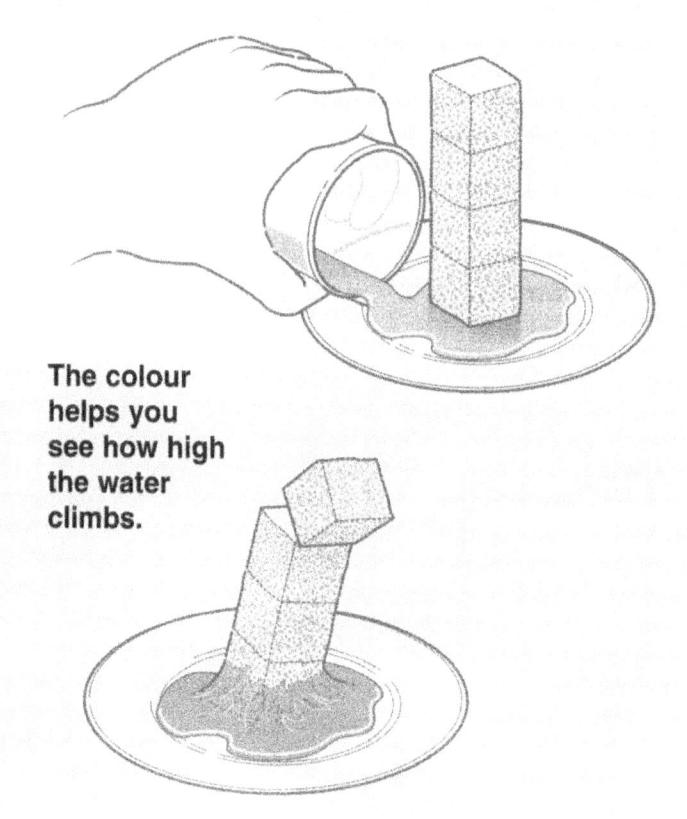

The water climbs up the tower as the dry sugar soaks it up. The tower falls over when the sugar gets soggy.

**The colour helps you see how high the water climbs.**

*Usborne Science Activities:
Science in the Kitchen*
Rebecca Heddle

1. How many sugar lumps do you need for this experiment?
   You need ..........................................

2. How do you make a tower with sugar lumps?
   You put ..........................................

3. How do you know how high the water climbs?
   You can see ......................................

4. What does **soggy** mean?
   cold    hard    wet
   **Soggy** means .................................

5. What happens when the sugar lumps get soggy?
   The tower ........................................

# Opposites using un

tidy

untidy

We can give some words an opposite meaning by writing **un** before them.

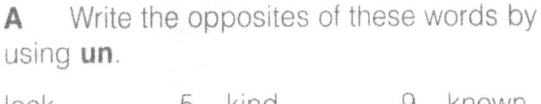

**A** Write the opposites of these words by using **un**.

1 lock
2 paid
3 well
4 pack
5 kind
6 do
7 screw
8 wind
9 known
10 tie
11 load
12 wrap

**B** Choose any six of the words you have made and use them in sentences of your own.

**C** Write out these sentences, adding **un** to the words in bold type so as to give them an opposite meaning.

1 It did not take Susan long to **dress**.
2 The room was very **tidy**.
3 This water is **fit** for drinking.
4 What he said was **true**.
5 The injured man was **able** to walk.
6 Tom sat in a corner looking very **happy**.
7 They were **willing** to go.
8 The bridge was **safe** for traffic.

37

# Opposites change of words

tall

short

The words **tall** and **short** are **opposite** in meaning.

| | |
|---|---|
| bad | good |
| big | small |
| cold | hot |
| early | late |
| empty | full |
| hard | soft |
| in | out |
| new | old |
| open | shut |
| strong | weak |
| tall | short |
| tame | wild |

Learn the pairs of opposites in the list on the left, then put the right word in each space in the sentences below.

1 Barry bought a new car and sold the ____ one.

2 We had a ____ day out even though the weather was bad.

3 I was late for school yesterday, but I was ____ today.

4 The lion is strong, but the mouse is ____ .

5 There was hot and ____ water in the bathroom.

6 Some apples are hard; others are ____ .

7 Mr. Wells was in, but Mrs. Wells was ____ .

8 Paul is a tall boy, but his brother Mark is quite ____ .

9 The shop is open on Saturday and ____ on Sunday.

10 Some horses are wild and some are ____ .

38

# Adding -ed to doing words

When we add **-ed** to verbs ending with **y** we change the **y** to **i**.

Change the **y** to **i**
Add on **-ed**

try
tr**i**
tr**ied**

marry
marr**i**
marr**ied**

With these words the **y** is changed to **i** and **-d** only is added.

pay    lay    say
paid   laid   said

I tidy my bedroom

I tidied my bedroom

**A** Add **-ed** to each of these words. Remember to change the **y** to **i**.

1  dry      4  tidy     7  hurry
2  carry    5  cry      8  fry
3  copy     6  bury     9  empty

**B** Use the words you have learnt to fill the spaces.

1  I ___ to catch the train.
2  We had ___ bacon and eggs for breakfast.
3  Janet ___ when she fell off the wall.
4  Keith ___ the heavy basket all the way home.
5  The sun and the wind soon ___ the washing.
6  Robert ___ the room after the party.
7  The dog ___ a bone in the garden.
8  Bill ___ the words in his notebook.
9  I ___ the butcher for the meat.

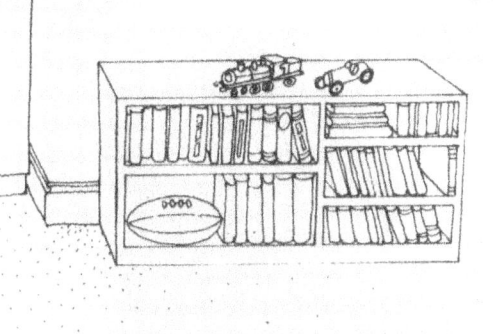

# Prepositions

off
behind
across
under
into

before
in
on
over
near

Use the words in the list on the left to fill the spaces in the sentences below.

1. Humpty fell ____ the wall.
2. The man dived ____ the pool. 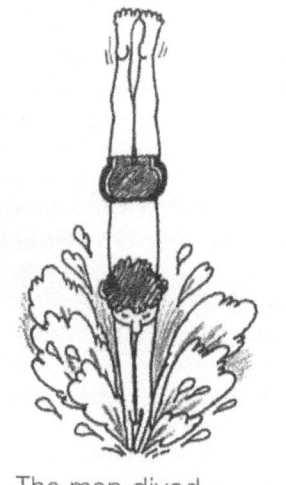
3. The horse jumped ____ the fence. 
4. The dog is ____ the table. 
5. The chicken is walking ____ the road. 
6. There is an apple ____ the plate. 
7. There are flowers ____ the vase. 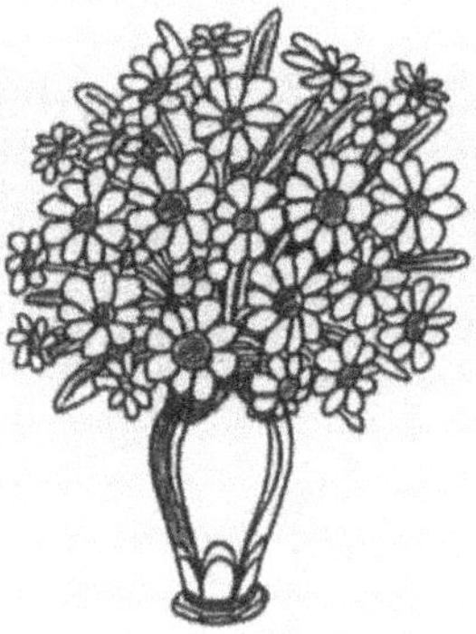
8. There is a guard ____ the fire. 
9. James is standing ____ the table.
10. John is hiding ____ the armchair.

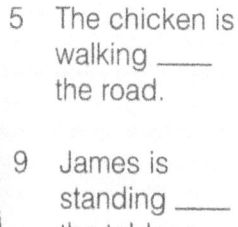

# Matching parts of sentences

Here you see two parts of a sentence.

        Jane went to bed early      because she was so tired.

The first part tells what Jane did.

The second part tells why she did it.

Each sentence below is in two parts, but the parts have become mixed up.

Write the first part of each sentence then add on the part which fits it.

| | | |
|---|---|---|
| 1 | The leaves were falling | a very long neck. |
| 2 | Tony and Sheila | is called a lamb. |
| 3 | The cat lapped up | go to the seaside. |
| 4 | Our baby likes | are brother and sister. |
| 5 | The rabbit has | is called a stable. |
| 6 | A baby sheep | from the trees. |
| 7 | People often catch cold | a short furry tail. |
| 8 | A giraffe has | all the milk in the dish. |
| 9 | The home of a horse | playing with his rattle. |
| 10 | In the summer many people | in very wet weather. |

41

# In the woods

Carol and her younger sister Mary went for a walk in the woods one day. They took their dog Sammy with them. Sammy ran on in front of them. He knew the way very well, for he had been there many times before.

The children found some bluebells growing in the woods, so they picked a bunch for their mother. While they were doing this, Sammy saw a rabbit sitting under a tree. He barked loudly and ran after it. But he did not catch it, for the rabbit ran into a hole in the ground.

True or false?

1. Carol is older than Mary.
2. Sammy catches a rabbit.
3. Sammy has been to these woods before.
4. The rabbit barks when it sees Sammy.
5. Sammy gets stuck in a rabbit hole.
6. The children pick flowers for their mother.
7. The rabbit chases Sammy.
8. Mary and Carol pick a lot of primroses.
9. Carol and Mary are sisters.
10. **Catch** rhymes with **watch**.

# Conjunctions using and

Read these two sentences.

Simon is going fishing.
I am going fishing.

We can join these sentences by using **and**. **And** is a conjunction.

Simon **and** I are going fishing.

Here are more joined sentences.

John is tall.
John is strong.

John is tall **and** strong.

Marva put her toys away.
She went to bed.

Marva put her toys away **and** went to bed.

Use **and** to join each pair of sentences below.

1. Our cat is white.
   Our cat is fluffy.

2. The room was clean.
   The room was tidy.

3. Grandpa sat in the armchair.
   He fell fast asleep.

4. The day was fine.
   The day was warm.

5. I gave the newsagent fifty pence.
   I had five pence change.

6. The farmer ploughs the fields.
   He sows the seed.

7. We went to the park.
   We played ball.

8. The nurse took my temperature.
   The nurse took my pulse.

9. John had his breakfast.
   John went to school.

# Things we eat and drink

Our milkman brings us a **bottle** of milk every day.

We can buy a **loaf** of bread from the baker.

Copy the words below and fill in the gaps. The words you need are in exercise B.

**A**

1  a bunch of ____
2  a bar of ____
3  a tin of ____
4  a bottle of ____

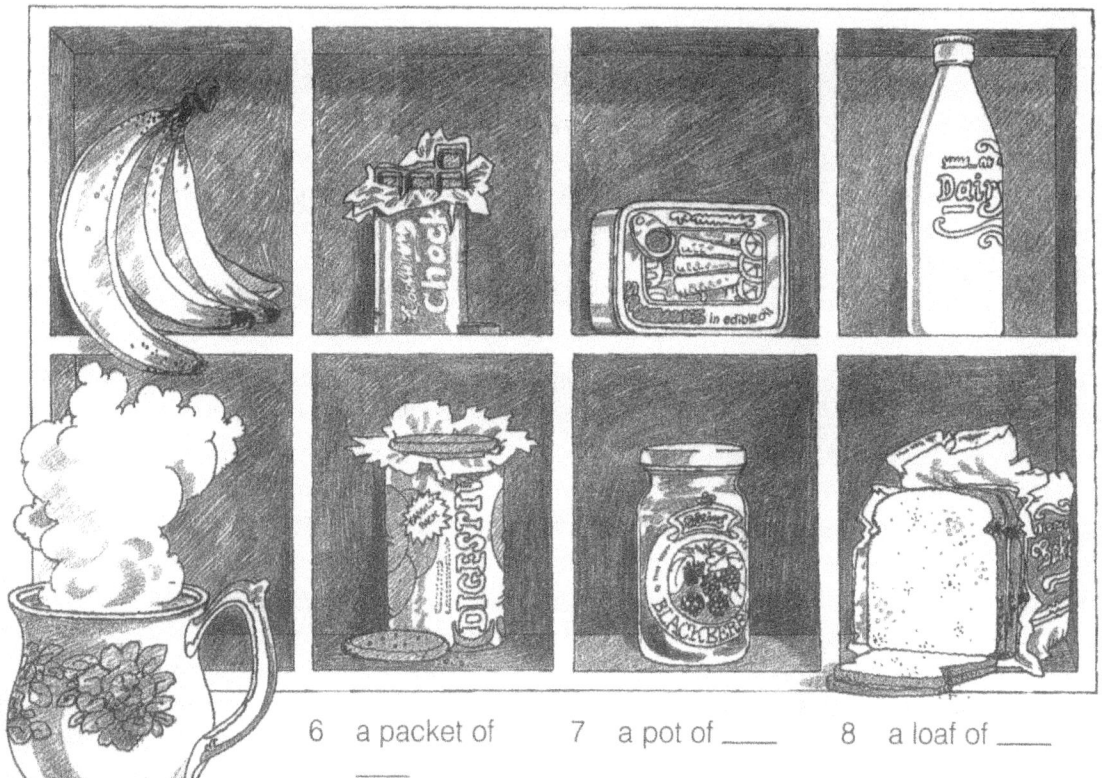

5  a cup of ____
6  a packet of ____
7  a pot of ____
8  a loaf of ____

**B**  What are the missing words?

1  a ____ of biscuits
2  a ____ of bread
3  a ____ of jam
4  a ____ of tea
5  a ____ of milk
6  a ____ of bananas
7  a ____ of chocolate
8  a ____ of sardines

# Rhymes

### The Vulture

The vulture eats between his meals,
And that's the reason why
He very, very rarely feels
As well as you or I.

His eye is dull, his head is bald,
His neck is growing thinner.
Oh! What a lesson for us all
To only eat at dinner!

*Hilaire Belloc*


**A**

1  Which word rhymes with **why**?

2  Which word rhymes with **feels**?

3  Write the word which rhymes with **thinner**.

4  Do the words **bald** and **all** rhyme?


**B**  Write two words which rhyme with each of the words in bold type. The sentences will help you to find them.

**snow**　　James had a ___ and arrow.
　　　　　　We looked high and ___ for the bat.

**flight**　　Jill had all her sums ___ .
　　　　　　She goes to bed early every ___ .

**tree**　　Robert fell down and cut his ___ .
　　　　　　He was away from school for ___ days.

**knows**　　Mr. Gardener ___ lovely roses.
　　　　　　He ___ them to all his friends.

# Using has and have

For **one** person or thing we use **has**.

For **more than one** person or thing we use **have**.

Always use **have** with **I** or **you**.

Our cat **has** kittens.
Uncle Ben **has** bought a new car.

The monkeys **have** long tails.
The children **have** gone to the circus.

I **have** a bad cold.
You **have** grown quite a lot.

**A** Write **has** or **have** in each space.

1 Simon _____ lost his dinner money.
2 Where _____ you been all day?
3 The books _____ been left out.
4 The book _____ been left out.
5 _____ Dad come home yet?
6 _____ the children come home yet?
7 Both the kittens _____ grey fur.
8 _____ the postman called?
9 The elephant _____ a long trunk.
10 Elephants _____ long trunks.

**B** Write three sentences of your own using **has**, and three using **have**.

**C** Add beginnings to these sentences.

1 ............................. has a bad temper.
2 ............................. have muddy shoes.
3 ............................. has eaten all the cake.
4 ............................. have worked hard.
5 ............................. has satellite television.

# Words with more than one meaning

Some words have more than one meaning.

Mind you do not **drop** that plate.

There is not a **drop** of milk left.

back
band
calf
lean
left
mine
post
stick
suit

Use the words in the list on the left to fill these spaces. The same word must be used for each pair of sentences.

1. My ____ is bad after weeding the garden.
   I will be ____ in half an hour.

2. A ____ is a young cow.
   The back of the leg below the knee is called the ____ .

3. A new ____ was put up to hold the clothes line.
   Would you like me to ____ your letter?

4. Please don't ____ against the glass door.
   This beef is very ____ .

5. Coal is dug out of a ____ .
   Your bat is much better than ____ .

6. The ____ played a lively tune.
   Gloria's hair was tied back with an elastic ____ .

7. George writes with his ____ hand.
   There are only two pears ____ in the dish.

8. Will you ____ a stamp on this envelope?
   He used a short ____ to make a fishing rod.

9. James wore his new grey ____ to the wedding.
   Alison's new dress does not ____ her at all.

47

# Going to school

John Dawes and his sister Ann go to the same school. John is two years older than Ann. He is in Class 3 and Ann is in Class 1.

The school is quite near their home and so they walk there each day. Before breakfast John takes his dog, Bobby, for a long walk and Ann feeds her two rabbits, Snowy and Sooty.

John and Ann often meet their friends on the way to school and they always say hallo to Mrs. Davies the lollipop lady.

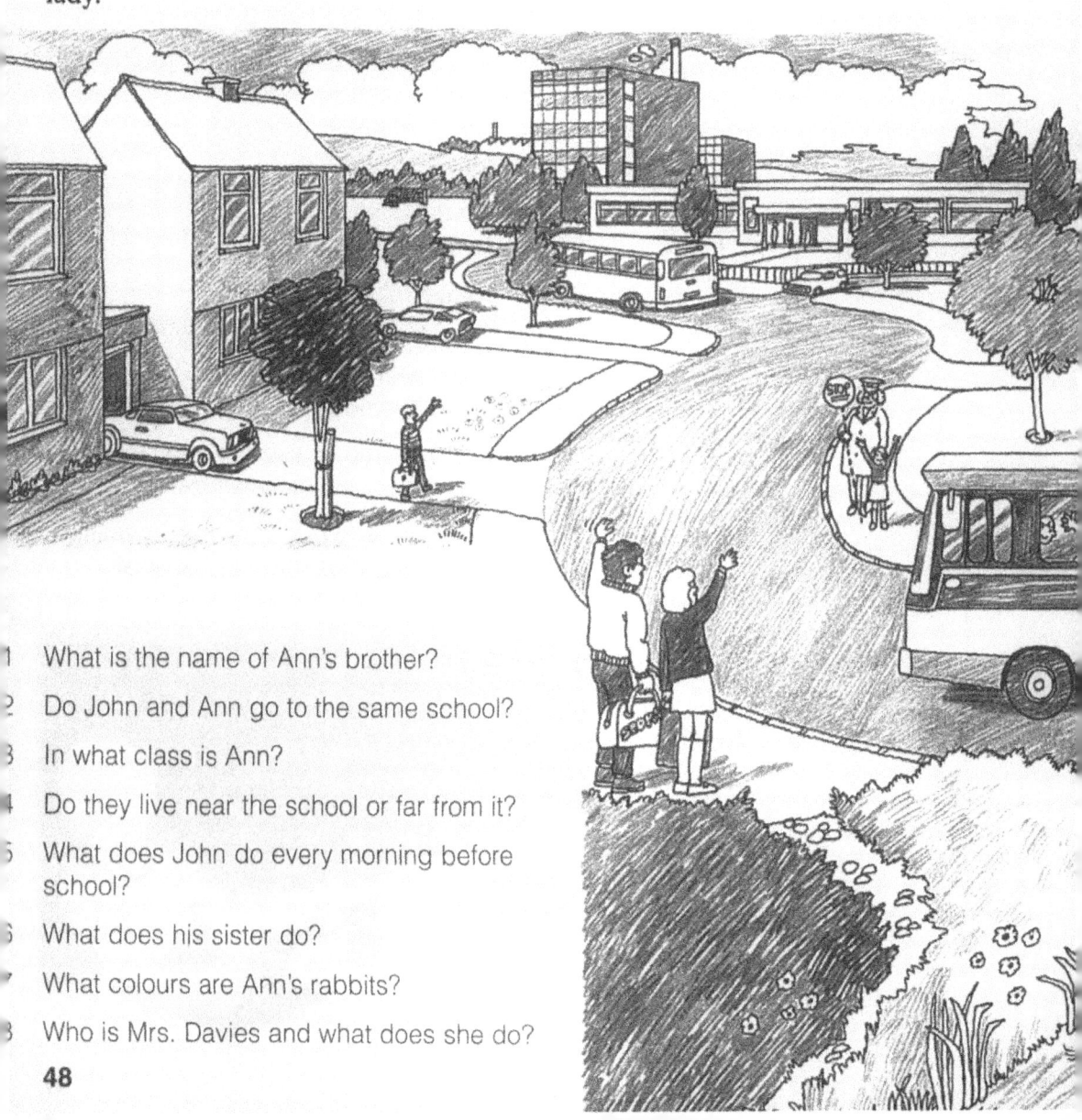

1. What is the name of Ann's brother?
2. Do John and Ann go to the same school?
3. In what class is Ann?
4. Do they live near the school or far from it?
5. What does John do every morning before school?
6. What does his sister do?
7. What colours are Ann's rabbits?
8. Who is Mrs. Davies and what does she do?

# Same sound – different meaning

Some words have the same sound as other words, but they are different in spelling and in meaning.

Look at these four pairs of words.

**one** — You have **one** nose and one mouth.
**won** — Jack **won** a prize for good writing.

**by** — He was standing **by** the door.
**buy** — I will **buy** you a bar of chocolate.

**made** — The toy was **made** in England.
**maid** — The **maid** dusted the chairs.

**tale** — A **tale** is a story.
**tail** — The squirrel has a bushy **tail**.

Choose the right word from the pair above to fill each space.

1 **one    won**
   Wilson ____ the race easily.

2 **tale    tail**
   Paul read a fairy ____ to Janet.

3 **by    buy**
   I am going to ____ some sweets.

4 **one    won**
   There was only ____ apple left.

5 **made    maid**
   Penny ____ a dress for herself.

6 **tale    tail**
   Our dog wags his ____ when he is happy.

7 **by    buy**
   The family went to London ____ train.

8 **made    maid**
   The new ____ tidied the bedrooms in the hotel.

# People who work

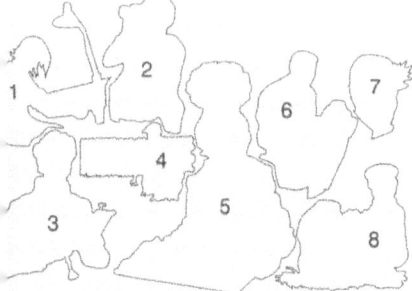

**A** Use the words in the list to name each person. Number your words from 1 to 8 as in the pictures.

baker
butcher
doctor
architect
farmer
photographer
cashier
miner
pilot
dentist
zoo keeper

**B** Who am I?

1 I am trained to look after your teeth.
2 You buy meat from me.
3 I try to cure you when you are ill.
4 I work at the check-out in a supermarket.
5 I dig coal from the earth.
6 I look after lots of different animals.
7 I fly aeroplanes all over the world.
8 I make bread, buns and cakes.
9 I use my camera in my work.
10 I design buildings and draw plans.

# The not words

We sometimes join **not** to another word.

When we do this we leave out the **o** in **not** and write ' in its place.

*Examples*

| is not | isn't |
| was not | wasn't |
| does not | doesn't |
| has not | hasn't |
| are not | aren't |
| were not | weren't |
| do not | don't |
| have not | haven't |

Remember that the ' must go where the **o** was.

**A** Join each pair of words together.

1. does not
2. were not
3. has not
4. is not
5. have not
6. was not
7. do not
8. are not

**B** Write these sentences, using one word in place of the two words in bold type in each line.

1. The cuckoo **does not** make a nest of its own.
2. The twins **were not** in school today.
3. Dad **has not** gone to work yet.
4. This milk **is not** fresh.
5. **Was not** that a dainty dish to set before the king?
6. Some children **do not** have dinner at school.
7. We **have not** had the treat we were promised.
8. These oranges **are not** very sweet.

**C** Join these words together.

1. did not
2. could not
3. had not
4. would not
5. should not

51

# Using do and does

We use **does** when we speak of **one person or thing**.

We use **do** when we speak of **more than one**.

Always use **do** with **you**, even for one person.

Always use **do** with **I**.

| One | More than one |
|---|---|
| I do | we do |
| you do | you do |
| he, she, it does | they do |

**A** Fill each space with **do** or **does**.

1 Martin ____ his exercises every morning.
2 Many people ____ exercises to keep fit.
3 I hope you ____ well in the test.
4 Our dog ____ like a meaty bone.
5 Susan and I ____ our homework together.
6 Henry ____ his best to keep the garden tidy.

**B** **Don't** and **doesn't** follow the same rules.

Write **don't** or **doesn't** in each space.

1 We ____ go to bed very early in summer.
2 The shop ____ close till six o'clock.
3 Jane ____ like washing up.
4 You will miss the bus if you ____ hurry.
5 I ____ go to the cinema very often.
6 Colin ____ want any breakfast this morning.

# Capital letters

Capital letters are used –

1 to begin a sentence

2 for the names of people and pets

3 for the names of places, rivers, mountains and so on

4 for the names of the days of the week and months of the year

**A** There are **fourteen words** in this list which should begin with a capital letter. Write them in the order in which they come.

| fine | france | monday |
| london | shoes | england |
| plate | nelson | jones |
| moscow | kenya | table |
| bread | banana | arthur |
| friday | ahmed | chest |
| thomson | april | paper |
| apple | chicken | july |

**B** Write these sentences in your book. Use **capital letters** where they are needed.

1 did you know that i was seven last sunday?

2 harjit and bela live in church street.

3 roy goes to brighton every saturday.

4 i take my dog chum for a walk every day.

5 jack and jill went up the hill.

6 farmer grey has a cow named daisy.

7 we shall be flying to paris next tuesday.

8 the severn is the longest river in england.

# Caterpillar

Once a chubby caterpillar
Sat upon a leaf,
Singing, "Eat, eat and be merry –
Life is very brief."

Soon he lost his appetite
And changed his merry tune.
He started spinning, hid himself
Inside a hard cocoon.

And he was still and quiet there –
Day after day went by.
At last it cracked and he emerged,
A gorgeous butterfly.

He spread his brown and crimson wings
And warmed them in the sun
And sang, "Now I must see the world –
My life has just begun."

*Wendy Cope*

Copy the sentences. Fill in the spaces.

1   The word ___ tells us that the caterpillar is quite fat.

2   Another word for **brief** with five letters is _____.

3   The caterpillar makes his cocoon by ___.

4   The caterpillar changes into a ___.

5   ___ is another word for **crimson**.

# Joining words

Some words are made by joining two words together.

**arm + chair = armchair**

**A** The names of things you see in the pictures are made in this way. Copy them from the list on the left.

birdcage
cupboard
eggcup
flowerpot
snowman
tablecloth
teapot
wallpaper

**B** Join the two words in bold type in each phrase to make one word, starting with the second word.

*Example* 1 headache

1 An **ache** in your **head**
2 A **mill** which is worked by the **wind**
3 The land at the **side** of the **sea**
4 A **bin** in which **dust** is put
5 A **shoe** for a **horse**
6 A **bag** carried in the **hand**
7 A **paper** in which **news** is printed
8 A **room** for a **bed**
9 A **ball** game which is played with the **foot**
10 The **bell** on a **door**

55

# Verbs past time

We do not always add **-ed** to verbs to show **past time**.

|  | Now | Past |
|---|---|---|
|  | Today I **fly**. | Yesterday I **flew**. |
|  | Today I **come**. | Last week I **came**. |

Learn the words in the list, then do the exercises.

| Present | Past |
|---|---|
| bite | bit |
| break | broke |
| come | came |
| creep | crept |
| do | did |
| draw | drew |
| drink | drank |
| fall | fell |
| fly | flew |
| give | gave |
| hide | hid |
| wear | wore |

**A** Copy these columns. Fill the blanks.

| | Present | Past | | Present | Past |
|---|---|---|---|---|---|
| 1 | draw | ___ | 7 | ___ | broke |
| 2 | drink | ___ | 8 | ___ | hid |
| 3 | bite | ___ | 9 | ___ | crept |
| 4 | fly | ___ | 10 | do | ___ |
| 5 | ___ | came | 11 | ___ | fell |
| 6 | ___ | wore | 12 | give | ___ |

**B** Put the right word in each space.

1 Zek ___ the ball in the drawer.   **hide**
2 Mrs. Dobbs ___ Sam a flapjack.   **give**
3 The robin ___ away when we got near.   **fly**
4 A big dog ___ Susan on the leg.   **bite**
5 Who ___ this lovely picture?   **draw**
6 The football ___ the window.   **break**
7 Philip ___ his best writing.   **do**
8 Jill ___ her new shoes yesterday.   **wear**

# Opposites change of word

Learn this list of opposites, then answer the questions.

| | |
|---|---|
| begin | finish |
| bottom | top |
| clean | dirty |
| down | up |
| dry | wet |
| fresh | stale |
| give | take |
| high | low |
| over | under |
| pretty | ugly |
| right | wrong |
| thick | thin |

**A** Write the opposites of these words.

1  ugly
2  thin
3  wrong
4  under
5  stale
6  take
7  down
8  bottom
9  dirty
10  finish
11  dry
12  high

**B** Copy these sentences. In each space write the opposite of the word in bold type.

1  Simon rode **up** the lane, then ____ again.

2  The show will **begin** at 7 o'clock and ____ at 9 o'clock.

3  The **clean** plates were put away and the ____ ones were put in the sink.

4  The ____ of the pole was thicker than the **top**.

5  Three sums were **right** and one was ____ .

6  The baker had no **fresh** loaves, only ____ ones.

7  Please **take** this tea away and ____ me some milk.

8  Tim jumped **over** the bar. David ducked ____ it.

9  Jeremy likes **thick** slices of bread. Jean only eats ____ slices.

10  Sally looks **pretty** when she smiles but ____ when she frowns.

# Same sound – different meaning

Look at the four pairs of words below.

The words in each pair have the same sound but are different in spelling and meaning.

| | |
|---|---|
| **not** | Mrs. Young was **not** at home. |
| **knot** | There was a **knot** in the rope. |
| **new** | The **new** car is faster than the old one. |
| **knew** | Richard **knew** all the songs the class sang. |
| **sea** | Several ships were sailing on the **sea**. |
| **see** | We **see** with our eyes. |
| **our** | **Our** things are the things that belong to us. |
| **hour** | There are sixty minutes in an **hour**. |

Fill each space with the right word.

1. Henry wore his ____ blazer to school.
2. The boat was wrecked in the stormy ____ .
3. I did ____ eat the apple because it was bad.
4. Jenny ____ her tables well.
5. We put ____ books under the desks.
6. From the top of the tower we could ____ the ____ .
7. James could ____ untie the ____ in his shoelace.
8. The schoolchildren get an ____ for lunch.

# Collections

Look at the words used for each collection below.

We call a number of sheep together a **flock**.

A   Use the pictures to help you fill in the gaps.

1   a box of ____

2   a crowd of ____

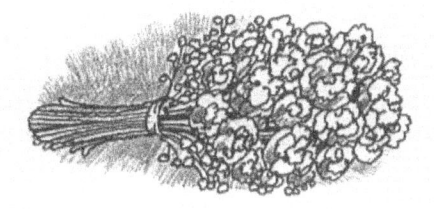

3   a bunch of ____

4   a clump of ____

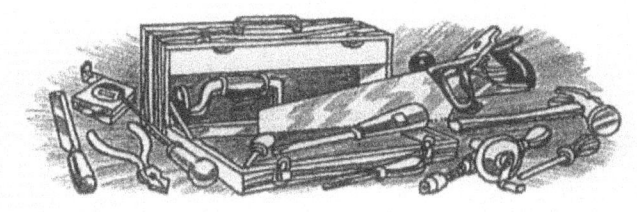

5   a pack of ____

6   a set of ____

8   a flock of ____

7   a herd of ____

B   What are the missing words?

1   a ____ of flowers
2   a ____ of elephants
3   a ____ cards
4   a ____ of people
5   a ____ of sheep
6   a ____ of trees
7   a ____ of chocolates
8   a ____ of tools

59

# Jane's new bicycle

Jane has a brand new bicycle. It was given to her by her Uncle Bob as a present on her seventh birthday.

The bicycle is painted bright orange. Behind the seat is a black, plastic saddle-bag and there is a large, shiny bell on the handlebars.

Every evening Jane rides her bicycle down the lane behind her house. She goes to meet her father on his way home from work.

1   Who gave Jane the new bicycle?

2   How old was she when she was given the new bicycle?

3   Where is the saddle-bag?

4   What is the saddle-bag made of?

5   What is on the handlebars?

6   How often does Jane ride the bicycle?

7   Where is the lane where Jane rides?

8   Why does she ride down the lane in the evening?

# Showing ownership

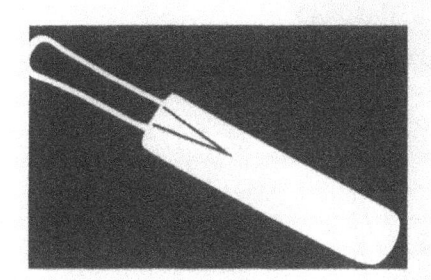

This is Imran's bat.

The **'s** shows that Imran **owns** the bat.

Look at these pictures.

See who **owns** each thing.

Write **'s** after each child's name to finish the exercise. The first is done for you.

1  Imran
2  Sarah 
3  Ann 
4  Oku 
5  Sean 
6  Jade 
7  David 
8  Ernestine 

Copy these in your book.

1  Imran's bat
2  ____ teddy bear
3  ____ ball
4  ____ top
5  ____ car
6  ____ pram
7  ____ scooter
8  ____ cat

# Groups

A pansy is a **flower**.   A cat is an **animal**.   A rook is a **bird**.   A fir is a **tree**.

**A**  Draw four columns in your book like these. Then put the words below in their proper places.

| Animals | Birds | Trees | Flowers |
|---------|-------|-------|---------|
|         |       |       |         |

| | | | |
|---|---|---|---|
| beech | thrush | oak | fir |
| robin | dog | cow | rose |
| tulip | daisy | lark | goat |
| sheep | rook | pansy | elm |

**B**  Draw these four columns in your book. Put the words in their proper places.

| Tools | Clothes | Furniture | Colours |
|-------|---------|-----------|---------|
|       |         |           |         |

| | | | |
|---|---|---|---|
| table | coat | yellow | axe |
| spanner | hammer | shorts | wardrobe |
| green | shirt | jersey | saw |
| chair | settee | blue | brown |

# Similars

Some words mean much the same as other words:

A **large** house
A **big** house

The words **large** and **big** are **similar**, or **alike**, in meaning.

Learn these similars, then do the exercises.

| | |
|---|---|
| creep | crawl |
| finish | end |
| halt | stop |
| large | big |
| present | gift |
| speak | talk |
| start | begin |
| stout | fat |
| tear | rip |
| tug | pull |

**A** In place of each word in bold type write a word which has a **similar** meaning.

1 I **start** work at eight o'clock.
2 Lizards **creep** along the ground.
3 John gave Jane's hair a playful **tug**.
4 A **large** crowd saw a fine game.
5 They do not **speak** to each other now.
6 Cars must **halt** at the crossroads.
7 The cook was a **stout** person.
8 There is a **tear** in my coat.
9 Carol had a lovely **present** from her aunt.
10 Our holiday will **finish** next Sunday.

**B** For each word below write one which is similar in meaning.

1 big
2 talk
3 end
4 pull
5 gift
6 crawl
7 stop
8 begin

**C** Use your dictionary to help you find words similar in meaning to these words.

1 colossal   h _ _ _
2 bouquet   b _ _ _ _
3 demonstrate   s _ _ _
4 precious   v _ _ _ _ _ _ _
5 applaud   c _ _ _

63

# Adjectives

The rabbit has **long** ears.

The word **long** tells **what kind** of ears the rabbit has. **Long** describes the rabbit's ears.

Words that describe nouns are called adjectives.

fast
gold
tasty
kind
shady
sour
savage
silk
blazing
rough

**A** Choose one of the words in the list on the left to describe each of the things below.

1  a ____ dog          6  a ____ fire
2  a ____ tree         7  a ____ meal
3  a ____ sea          8  a ____ car
4  a ____ ring         9  a ____ friend
5  a ____ blouse      10  a ____ apple

**B** Now use the best adjective you can think of for each of these words.

1  a ____ boy          5  a ____ field
2  a ____ wind         6  a ____ flower
3  a ____ dress        7  a ____ kitten
4  a ____ policeman    8  a ____ orange

**C** Fill each gap with a suitable noun.

1  a lovely ____       5  a quiet ____
2  a naughty ____      6  a clean ____
3  a sunny ____        7  a clever ____
4  a wide ____         8  a wild ____

# Same sound – different meaning

Look at the four pairs of words below.

The words in each pair have the same sound but are different in spelling and meaning.

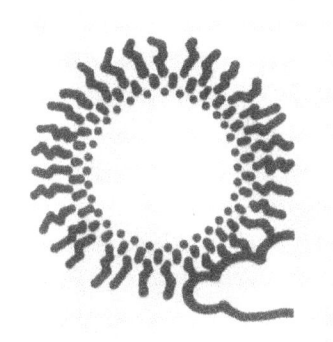

son    Mr. Day has one **son** and one daughter.

sun    The **sun** rises in the east and sets in the west.

weak    The sick man was too **weak** to get up.

week    There are seven days in a **week**.

hair    **Hair** grows on your head.

hare    A **hare** is an animal very much like a rabbit.

pair    A **pair** is a set of two, like a pair of shoes.

pear    A **pear** is a sweet juicy fruit.

Fill each space with the right word.

1. Dad bought a new ____ of shoes.
2. The heat of the ____ makes plants grow.
3. The woman had black curly ____ .
4. The school was closed for a ____ .
5. This ____ is not quite ripe.
6. The ____ has long ears and a short tail.
7. Mary was quite ____ after her long illness.
8. The farmer told his ____ to fetch a pitchfork.

# Making a snowman

A short time ago David and his friends John and Peter made a fine snowman. First they made a very big snowball for the head. Then David got a shovel and made a huge pile of snow for the body. Next, John and Peter put the head on top of the body. For eyes they used two bits of coal, and for the nose they used a carrot. Then Peter cut a long slit for the mouth.

John stuck an old clay pipe in the snowman's mouth, and Peter put an old bowler hat on its head. When they had finished making him they named him Sammy Snowball.

1  Which part of the snowman did the boys make first?
2  How did David make the body?
3  Who put the head on the body?
4  What did they use for eyes?
5  What was the carrot used for?
6  What did John stick in the snowman's mouth?
7  What did Peter put on the snowman's head?
8  Look at the picture and describe what is happening.

66

# Conjunctions using but

Read these two sentences.

Karen dropped her clock.
It did not break.

We can join these sentences by using **but**.
**But** is a conjunction.

Karen dropped her clock **but** it did not break.

See how these other sentences are joined.

Paul fell down.
He did not cry.

Paul fell down **but** he did not cry.

The dog chased a rabbit.
He did not catch it.

The dog chased a rabbit **but** he did not catch it.

Use **but** to join each pair of sentences below.

1. Elsa looked for her lost book.
   She could not find it.

2. We hoped to go out.
   It was too wet.

3. Tim fell off his scooter.
   He did not hurt himself.

4. The postman rang the bell.
   He could not get an answer.

5. They hurried to the station.
   The train had gone.

6. Preshani felt ill.
   She did not want to stay in bed.

7. Ann wanted a chocolate.
   The box was empty.

8. I longed for some ice-cream.
   I had no money.

9. We went into the park.
   We did not stay long.

# Rhymes

**A** Write this poem in your book.
Use the words in the list on the left to fill the spaces.

### Sleep

feet      night
sack      still
back      alight
will      street

In the dark and lonely ____ ,
When the stars are all ____ ,
Sleep comes creeping up the ____ ,
With her naked, silent ____ ,
Carrying upon her ____ ,
Dreams of all kinds in a ____ ;
Though the doors are bolted, ____
She can enter where she ____ ,
And she lingers, it is said,
Longest by the children's bed;
Smooths their pillows, strokes their curls,
Happy little boys and girls!

**B** How many rhyming words can you make by changing the first letter of each word below?

1   bed      4   try
2   back     5   kind
3   night    6   dark

# Using did and done

Pam **did** all the work.

Pam **has done** all the work.

(**has** helps the word **done**)

All the work **was done** by Pam.

(**was** helps the word **done**)

The word **did** needs no helping word.

The word **done** always has a helping word:

has done
have done
is done
are done
was done
were done
had done

**A** Use **did** or **done** to fill each space.

1 I ____
2 You have ____
3 It was ____
4 He ____
5 You ____
6 He has ____
7 We ____
8 They are ____
9 She ____
10 We had ____

**B** Fill each space with **did** or **done**.

1 Sally ____ her best to finish her homework.
2 We have ____ some good work today.
3 The soldier ____ his duty.
4 This drawing was ____ by Robert.
5 Robert ____ this drawing himself.
6 Have you ____ your homework?
7 Stephen ____ his homework after tea.
8 When I was ill Jean ____ the cooking.
9 Polly ____ some gardening and then she went out.
10 After Polly had ____ some gardening she went out.

**C** Add beginnings to these sentences.

1 .............................. done very well.
2 ................... did exactly what she was told.
3 ........ done the washing-up before I got home.
4 ......................... did just what he wanted.
5 ............. done far better than we expected.

**69**

# Putting sentences in order

Here are four short stories.
The sentences in them are in the wrong order.
Write them as they should be.

1    a    He paid the shopkeeper.
     b    He joined his friends outside.
     c    James went into the sweet shop.
     d    He put the change in his pocket.
     e    He asked for a packet of mints.

2    a    Suddenly there was a loud bang.
     b    He drove slowly into town.
     c    Mr. Warren's car was badly damaged.
     d    Mr. Warren left home at eight o'clock.
     e    He had crashed into the car in front.

3    a    He went to the bathroom to wash himself.
     b    He went off to catch the school bus.
     c    He ate his breakfast and left the table.
     d    He dressed himself and went downstairs.
     e    Michael got out of bed at eight o'clock.

4    a    They walked about collecting moon rocks.
     b    The rocket took off from the moon with a loud blast from its engines.
     c    Two spacemen climbed out of the rocket.
     d    The rocket landed safely on the moon.
     e    The spacemen climbed back into their rocket.

# Conjunctions using because, and, but

The word **because** can be used to join two sentences. **Because** is a conjunction.

*Example*

The dog bit John.
He was teasing it.
              *two sentences*

The dog bit John **because** he was teasing it.
              *one sentence*

**A**    Use **because** to join these sentences.

1   Liam was very happy.
    He was on holiday.

2   He did not drink his tea.
    It was cold.

3   Ben was excited.
    He was going to Disneyland.

**B**    Use **and** to join these sentences.

1   Peter dropped the cup.
    It broke.

2   Rajiv went into the park.
    He had a ride on the swing.

3   Alison opened the door.
    She crept in.

**C**    Use **but** to join these sentences.

1   It was a lovely hat.
    It was too small for Penny.

2   We waited for Anna.
    She did not turn up.

3   Felix wants to buy a bicycle.
    He hasn't got enough money.

**D**    Write the missing word **and**, **but** or **because** in each sentence.

1   Michael wanted to swim \_\_\_\_ his mother said it was too cold.

2   Sophie made the cakes \_\_\_\_ put them in the oven.

3   Zara went to bed early \_\_\_\_ she was not feeling well.

# In the garden

Penny and Philip Hall often help their parents in the garden. Penny digs up the weeds which grow among the plants with a small fork. She puts them in a wheelbarrow. When the wheelbarrow is full, Philip wheels it down the path to the bottom of the garden. Then he throws all the weeds on a big heap to be burnt by his father.

Every Saturday Mrs. Hall cuts the lawn with a mower and trims the hedges with a pair of shears. She also likes to look after the flowers. When they are in bloom she often picks some and puts them in vases in the house. Mr. Hall grows all the vegetables. These include potatoes, carrots, cabbages and runner beans.

1 How often does Mrs. Hall cut the grass?
2 Look carefully at the picture. How can you tell Mrs. Hall uses an electric mower?
3 Who likes digging up the weeds?
4 Which tool is used for trimming the hedges?
5 What is a **vase**?
6 Where does Mr. Hall have a bonfire?
7 What vegetables does Mr. Hall grow?
8 How does Philip help in the garden?

# Using commas in a list

When three or more nouns come together, we separate them by using **commas** (,).

*Example*
For tea we had cakes, jelly, fruit and trifle.

Notice that there is no comma between the last two things. The word **and** separates them.

**A** Copy these sentences. Put in the commas.

1 Robert Andrew Michael and Peter were ill.
2 The fishmonger had hake plaice herrings mackerel and cod.
3 London York Birmingham and Exeter are all cities.
4 The colours of the rainbow are red orange yellow green blue indigo and violet.
5 At the zoo we saw lions tigers elephants camels and monkeys.
6 You can play rounders netball tennis and cricket at the holiday club.
7 Shushana's mother brother sister and grandfather came to the school fête.
8 The fruit bowl was piled high with apples pears oranges grapes bananas and kiwi fruit.
9 Kate put her jeans a T-shirt and a warm sweater in her rucksack.
10 Mark carefully dried the forks knives and spoons.

**B** Finish these sentences with lists of your own. Use commas where they are needed and remember to put a full stop at the end of each sentence.

1 Mrs. Green bought . . . . . . . . . . . . . . . . . . . . . . . . . . .
2 My best friends are . . . . . . . . . . . . . . . . . . . . . . . . . . .
3 For his lunch Adam had . . . . . . . . . . . . . . . . . . . . . . .

# Where they live

**A** Learn the names of the homes of these creatures.

**Creature**   bee   bird   dog   horse   rabbit   spider

**Home**   hive   nest   kennel   stable   burrow   web

Write the missing words.

1  A ___ is the home of a spider.

2  The horse lives in a ___.

3  A ___ is a dog's home.

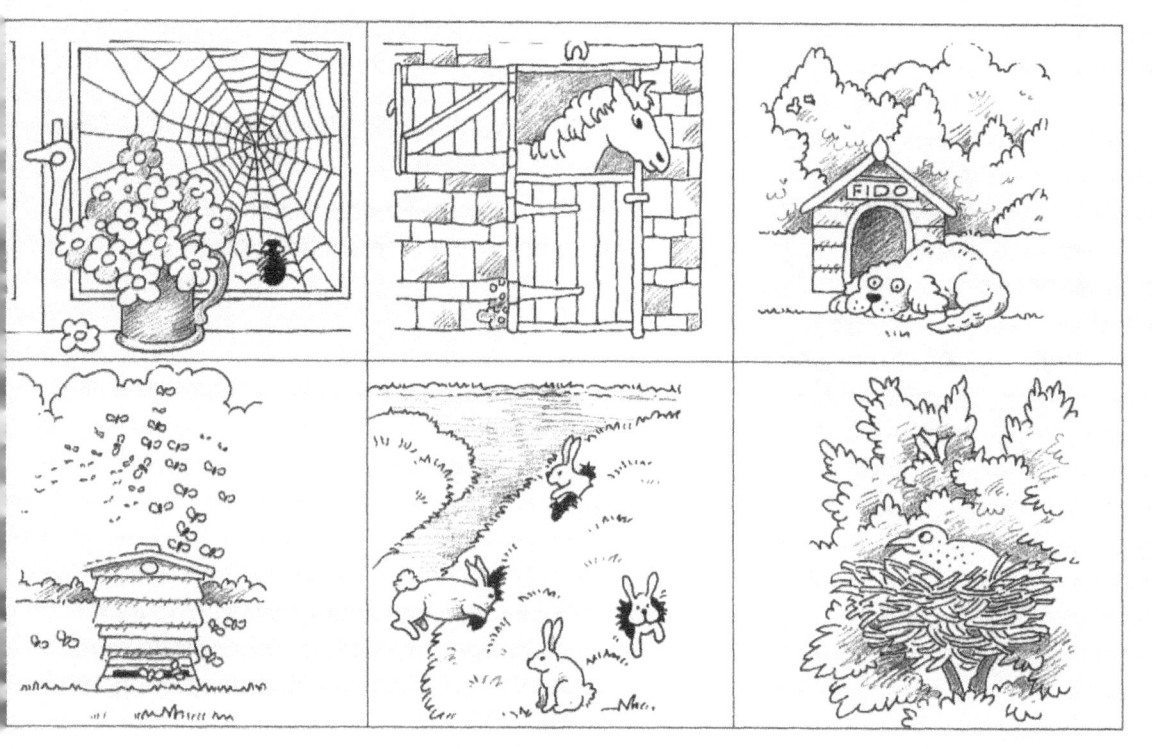

4  Bees live in a ___.

5  The rabbit lives in a ___.

6  A bird lives in a ___.

**B** Use your dictionary to find out which creatures live in these homes.

1  aviary

2  hutch

3  den

4  aquarium

5  byre

# Adjectives

**A** Use the words in the list on the left to describe the things below.

bright
fresh
happy
wooden
sharp
china
juicy
heavy

1 a ____ parcel
2 a ____ egg
3 a ____ star
4 a ____ teapot
5 a ____ knife
6 a ____ baby
7 a ____ orange
8 a ____ stool

**B** From the words in the list on the left choose the one which will best fit each line.

*Example*
1 The washing on the line is **clean**.
So the word **clean** fits line 1.

fine
stale
rich
clean
new
tidy
ripe
quiet

1 The washing on the line is ____ .
2 A pear which is ready for eating is ____ .
3 A person who has a lot of money is ____ .
4 A child who makes no noise is ____ .
5 A day when there is no rain is ____ .
6 Bread which was baked a week ago is ____ .
7 A dress which has never been worn is ____ .
8 A room in which nothing is out of place is ____ .

**C** Make up five sentences of your own using these words.

1 hungry
2 untidy
3 delicious
4 easy
5 sweet

# Hidden words

**A** Use a word of two letters to fill the gap in each of these sentences.

*Example*
1 At the seaside the children played in the s _ _ d.
*Answer* **an** s**an**d

1 At the seaside the children played in the s _ _ d.
2 The box was too heavy for Tom to l _ _ t.
3 The man struck a m _ _ ch to light his pipe.
4 Hot weather makes the butter very s _ _ t.
5 He did not have a w _ _ k of sleep last night.
6 Tony's coat was d _ _ p after the rain.
7 Martin caught a big f _ _ h with his new rod.
8 Six ducks were swimming on the p _ _ d.
9 Paul came l _ _ t in the race.
10 There were all s _ _ ts of toys in the shop.

**B** A word of three letters is hidden in each of the words in bold type. Find the ten words.

1 **grate**
an animal

2 **soaked**
a tree

3 **plant**
a small insect

4 **scarf**
we travel in it

5 **shears**
we listen with it

6 **scowl**
a big animal

7 **garment**
part of the body

8 **steal**
something to drink

9 **beggar**
we get it from a hen

10 **clipper**
a part of your mouth

# Using saw and seen

William **saw** a lion.

(**saw** needs no helping word)

William **had seen** a lion before.

(**had** helps the word **seen**)

We **have seen** lions at the zoo.

(**have** helps the word **seen**)

The word **saw** needs no helping word.

The word **seen** always has a helping word:

has seen
have seen
is seen
are seen
was seen
were seen
had seen

**A** Use **saw** or **seen** to fill each space.

1 She ____
2 They were : ____
3 I ____
4 She had ____
5 We ____
6 I have ____
7 They ____
8 It is ____
9 You ____
10 He was ____

**B** Which is right, **saw** or **seen**?

1 The wise men had ____ a bright star in the sky.
2 I ____ a giant at the fair.
3 Have you ____ the new car?
4 James ____ the football match from start to finish.
5 The policeman ____ a man breaking into a shop.
6 The robber was ____ by the policeman.
7 The robber did not know that he had been ____ .
8 I thought I ____ you at the party.
9 I knew I had ____ you before.
10 Crocuses are ____ in the spring.

# I saw a ship a-sailing

I saw a ship a-sailing,
   A-sailing on the sea;
And it was deeply laden
   With pretty things for me.

There were raisins in the cabin
   And almonds in the hold;
The sails were made of satin,
   And the mast was made of gold.

The four and twenty sailors
   Who stood upon the decks
Were four and twenty white mice
   With rings about their necks.

The captain was a fine plump duck
   With a jacket on his back,
And when the fairy ship set sail
   The captain he said Quack!

1. Where were the raisins?
2. What were the sails made of?
3. What part of the ship was made of gold?
4. How many sailors stood on the deck?
5. Who were the sailors?
6. Who was the captain?
7. What did he have on his back?
8. What did the captain say when the ship set sail?

# Rhymes

**A**  In each group below write four words which rhyme with the word in bold type. The first letter of each new word is given.

1 **bat**
h _ _
m _ _
c _ _
f _ _

2 **cap**
l _ _
t _ _
m _ _
r _ _

3 **din**
f _ _
w _ _
p _ _
b _ _

4 **rut**
c _ _
n _ _
b _ _
h _ _

5 **best**
v _ _ _
n _ _ _
r _ _ _
w _ _ _

6 **lash**
d _ _ _
m _ _ _
c _ _ _
s _ _ _

7 **tent**
b _ _ _
s _ _ _
l _ _ _
r _ _ _

8 **meat**
s _ _ _
h _ _ _
b _ _ _
n _ _ _

9 **lack**
p _ _ _
s _ _ _
r _ _ _
b _ _ _

**B**  Use a word which rhymes with **came** to fill the space in each sentence.

1 The horse was _ _ _ _ and could not run in the race.
2 The dog's _ _ _ _ was Bimbo.
3 Cricket is the _ _ _ _ I like best.
4 The candle _ _ _ _ _ is yellow.
5 The twins wear the _ _ _ _ kinds of clothes.
6 The keeper stroked the lion cub which was quite _ _ _ _ .
7 The _ _ _ _ _ of the picture was made of wood.
8 Judy took the _ _ _ _ _ for the broken window.

# Adjectives adding -er and -est

long

longer

longest

When we add **-er** or **-est** to a word ending with **e**, we drop the **e**.

wide

wider

widest

**A** Add **-er** or **-est** to the words in bold type to fill the spaces.

1 Andrew is much ____ than Derek. **tall**
2 The church is the ____ building in town. **high**
3 Carol has the ____ writing in the class. **neat**
4 In winter we wear the ____ clothes we have. **warm**
5 I am ____ than my brother James. **old**
6 This knife is ____ than yours. **sharp**

**B** Add **-er** or **-est** to the words in bold type to fill the gaps.

1 The weather is much ____ today. **fine**
2 This is the ____ jam I have ever tasted. **nice**
3 The pear was ____ than the banana. **ripe**
4 The old lion was the ____ of the lot. **tame**
5 King Solomon was the ____ of all men. **wise**
6 She is much ____ after her illness. **pale**

# Beginning and ending sentences

**A** Here are the beginnings of eight sentences. Finish each sentence yourself. Write them in your book.

1 The baby started crying ....................
2 The car was badly damaged ................
3 At the end of our street ....................
4 When tea was over ........................
5 The cawing of the rooks ...................
6 Mum sent for the doctor ...................
7 Jane fed the puppy ........................
8 The noise of the planes ...................

**B** Here are the endings of eight sentences. Write the first part of each in your own words.

1 ................ so he went to bed.
2 ................ and closed the door after him.
3 ................ because of the heavy rain.
4 ................ many trees lose their leaves.
5 ................ but could not do it.
6 ................ and put it in her purse.
7 ................ when her kitten got lost.
8 ................ and cut his knee.

# Similars

Some words mean much the same as other words.

A **wealthy** man
A **rich** man

The words **wealthy** and **rich** are **similar**, or **alike**, in meaning.

Learn these similars, then do the exercises.

| | |
|---|---|
| assist | help |
| broad | wide |
| correct | right |
| dwelling | home |
| farewell | goodbye |
| gaze | look |
| raise | lift |
| repair | mend |
| reply | answer |
| wealthy | rich |

**A** In place of each word in bold type, write a word which has a similar meaning.

1 The main street was very **broad**.
2 We stopped to **gaze** in the shop window.
3 Colin could hardly **raise** his arm.
4 The cobbler will **repair** my shoes today.
5 Will you **assist** me with my sums?
6 The duke is a very **wealthy** man.
7 William had all his sums **correct**.
8 The **reply** to the question was very short.
9 The shepherd's **dwelling** was a small cottage.
10 The sailor said **farewell** to his wife.

**B** For each word below write one which is similar in meaning. Use your dictionary or a thesaurus to help you.

1 difficult
2 chilly
3 sly
4 little
5 odour
6 remedy
7 terror
8 fatigue

# Two word games

**A** By writing the letter **s** before **pill** we make the word **spill**.

Write a letter before each word in bold type to make the word which fills the gap.

1. She wore ____ trousers at the party.  **ink**
2. The plate was too hot to ____ .  **old**
3. We watched the top ____ round and round.  **pin**
4. We ____ to read at school.  **earn**
5. The ____ of the ticket was fifty pence.  **rice**
6. The children made a sandcastle on the ____ .  **each**
7. Susan used a brush to ____ the path.  **weep**
8. An animal is sometimes called a ____ .  **east**

**B** From the letters in the word **rats** we can make the word **star**.

From the letters in the words in bold type make words which will fit into the spaces.

1. He could not ____ the heavy chest.  **flit**
2. Jean had a bruise on her ____ .  **inch**
3. The wind had blown every ____ off the tree.  **flea**
4. Philip came second in the sack ____ .  **care**
5. The oranges were twenty pence ____ .  **ache**
6. Colin clapped and cheered when his ____ won the cup.  **tame**
7. Anne was the ____ to go to bed.  **salt**
8. The children jumped ____ the stream.  **rove**

83

# Going for a picnic

One hot day in September Mr. and Mrs. Brown took their three children, Peter, Sally and Julie for a picnic in the woods.

While the children searched for conkers their parents put out cold sausages, potato salad and tins of Coke. Then Mrs. Brown opened a box of cakes she had made the day before.

Suddenly, there was a shriek from Julie. "Quick, Daddy! An adder!" she cried.

Mr. Brown sprang to his feet and ran to Julie. Then he laughed. "Don't worry, Julie," he said. "It's only a grass snake."

1   Where did the Brown family go for their picnic?
2   What did the children look for on the ground?
3   Why was Julie really frightened when she thought the grass snake was an adder?
4   Why is there no need to be frightened of a grass snake?
5   What did the Brown family have to eat on their picnic?
6   What did they have to drink?
7   Make a list of food you would take on a picnic.

# Things which are alike

When something is very **heavy** we say it is as **heavy** as **lead**.

This is because lead is a very, very heavy metal.

Learn the sayings in this list, then answer the questions opposite.

as cold as ice

as good as gold

as heavy as lead

as light as a feather

as quiet as a mouse

as slow as a snail

as sweet as honey

as thin as a rake

as warm as toast

as white as snow

**A**

1  as cold as ____
2  as white as ____
3  as good as ____
4  as warm as ____
5  as thin as a ____
6  as heavy as ____
7  as light as a ____
8  as sweet as ____
9  as quiet as a ____
10 as slow as a ____

**B**  Use the right word to finish each sentence.

1  The baby's toes were as ____ as toast.
2  The grapes were as ____ as honey.
3  David was as ____ as gold in school.
4  The tea was as ____ as ice.
5  Her hair was as ____ as snow.
6  The newspaper boy was as ____ as a snail.
7  This box is as ____ as a feather.
8  After his illness he was as ____ as a rake.

**C**  Make up some really good **new** sayings of your own.

1  as horrible as .................................
2  as frightening as .................................
3  as sharp as .................................
4  as comfortable as .................................
5  as happy as .................................

# Adjectives adding -er and -est

When we add **-er** or **-est** to some words we **double the last letter**.

big    bigger    biggest

When we add **-er** or **-est** to words ending with **y** we change the **y** to **i**.

easy    easier    easiest

**A**

Add **-er** or **-est** to the words in bold type to fill the spaces.

1  This is the ____ day for years.    **hot**
2  Holland is a ____ country than England.    **flat**
3  Friday was the ____ day of the week.    **wet**
4  Matthew picked the ____ slice of cake on the plate.    **big**
5  The clown's nose was ____ than a cherry.    **red**
6  It was the ____ day of his life.    **sad**

**B**

1  John is the ____ boy in the whole world.    **happy**
2  Ashley seems to be ____ than his brother.    **lazy**
3  The rose is a ____ flower than the dandelion.    **pretty**
4  Her bedroom is the ____ room in the house.    **tidy**
5  The boys are ____ than the girls.    **noisy**
6  Christmas is the ____ time of year.    **merry**
7  Your jokes are ____ than mine.    **funny**
8  Are toads ____ than frogs?    **slimy**
9  You will have to be ____ than this.    **early**
10 The ____ monster you ever saw in your life was trying to get in.    **hairy**

# Joining sentences using before

Read these two sentences.

We can join these sentences using **before**.

Claire cleaned her teeth.
She went to bed.

Claire cleaned her teeth **before** she went to bed.

**A** Use **before** to join each pair of sentences below.

1 Jake put on thick socks.
He pulled on his wellington boots.

2 Sam wrapped the present carefully.
He gave it to his mother.

3 Jo carefully looked left and right.
She crossed the road.

4 Kim said his prayers.
He fell asleep.

5 Think carefully.
Tell me the answer.

**B** Here are the beginnings to five sentences. Write the endings in your own words.

1 The dog barked twice before it ____ .

2 You must tidy your room before you ____ .

3 Wash your hands before you ____ .

4 You must pass your cycling proficiency test before you ____ .

5 My mother washed up before she ____ .

# Pronouns

a   I lent Paul a book and **Paul** lost **the book**.

b   I lent Paul a book and **he** lost **it**.

Instead of repeating the word **Paul**, the word **he** is used in **b**. Instead of repeating the words **the book**, the word **it** is used.

**A word which is used instead of a noun is called a pronoun.**

Look at these pronouns:

| | |
|---|---|
| I | me |
| you | you |
| he | him |
| she | her |
| it | it |
| we | us |
| they | them |

**A**   Rewrite these sentences, using **pronouns** in place of the nouns in bold type.

1   Alan told Jamie that **Alan** would help **Jamie**.

2   The rabbit ran away when **the rabbit** heard a dog barking.

3   Anne and Talika said that **Anne and Talika** would call again.

4   Mrs. Grey has two Siamese cats. **Mrs. Grey** adores **the Siamese cats**.

5   Marie promised June that **Marie** would feed the dog for **June**.

**B**   Write out these sentences and underline all the pronouns. There may not be pronouns in every sentence.

1   You always make me laugh.

2   David's mother said that he was feeling ill.

3   Ramu was tired after the walk.

4   Mum will be cross if we don't find the key.

5   We are lost.

6   Please tell me the truth.

7   You need three fillings.

8   Shaun is a very fast swimmer.

9   They will be here soon.

10   I lost it yesterday.

11   She is very sorry.

12   I saw you put it in the drawer.

# Looking back

**A** Write the **opposites** of:

1 top
2 full
3 late
4 pretty
5 wrong
6 tame
7 clean
8 fresh

**B** Write the words for **more than one**.

1 leaf
2 baby
3 box
4 wife
5 story
6 brush
7 coach
8 lady

**C** Add **-est** to each of these adjectives.

1 clean
2 big
3 happy
4 ripe
5 hot
6 long
7 fine
8 thin

**D** Name the **homes** of these creatures.

1 spider
2 rabbit
3 lion
4 robin
5 fish
6 dog
7 horse
8 bees

**E** Write words which are **similar** in meaning.

1 speak
2 broad
3 begin
4 wealthy
5 correct
6 stout
7 large
8 repair

**F** Write words which **sound** like these but have different spellings.

1 made
2 not
3 tail
4 won
5 by
6 see
7 our
8 new

89

# The summer holidays

Melly never liked the last day of summer term. Everyone else in Class 6 seemed to have exciting plans for the holidays. Melly's friend Anna was going to France. She said the sea was so blue there you could dive all day. Her friend Jane was going to work as a stable-hand in a real stables. She'd be allowed to ride the horses, too. Only Becca, who was younger than Melly and lived next door, was always in London when Melly came back from her fortnight at Grandma's.

*The Ghost Child*   Emma Tennant

1   Where does Melly live?
2   Who lives next door to Melly?
3   Where is Anna going on holiday?
4   Where is Jane going to work?
5   Which relation is Melly going to stay with?
6   How many weeks are there in a **fortnight**?
7   Do you feel sorry for Melly? Explain why you do or why you don't.

# Answers

## Page 1  The game of I spy

**A**
1. cup
2. peg
3. boat
4. sock
5. dog
6. log
7. tree
8. fish
9. jug
10. egg

**B**
1. egg
2. dog
3. fish
4. sock

## Page 2  Nouns

**A**
1. bed
2. pen
3. door
4. tap
5. lamp
6. book
7. drum
8. clock
9. spoon
10. bag

**B**
1. drum
2. bed
3. lamp
4. door
5. bag
6. book
7. tap
8. spoon
9. pen
10. clock

## Page 3  Using a and an

**A**
1. an eggcup
2. an axe
3. an arrow
4. an oven
5. an iron
6. an envelope
7. an apple
8. an onion

**B**
1. a clock
2. an armchair
3. an orchard
4. a book
5. a pen
6. an arch
7. a tree
8. a door
9. an elephant
10. an ostrich
11. an eagle
12. a hoop
13. a desk
14. an island
15. an umbrella

## Page 4  Numbers

**A**
1. three cats
2. eight flowers
3. two trees
4. ten eggs
5. seven bottles

**B**
1. thirteen
2. nineteen
3. eleven
4. fifteen
5. twelve
   fourteen
   sixteen
   eighteen

## Page 5 Verbs

**A**
1. washing
2. sleeping
3. fishing
4. eating
5. reading
6. jumping
7. flying
8. drinking

**B**
1. calling
2. drawing
3. doing
4. trying
5. pulling
6. seeing
7. hearing
8. raining
9. singing
10. barking
11. teaching
12. feeling

## Page 6 Pam's pet

1. Pam's cat is <u>black</u> in colour.
2. When Punch is happy, he <u>purrs</u>.
3. He uses his <u>tongue</u> to drink the milk.
4. Punch likes sitting by the <u>fire</u>.
5. He washes his face with his <u>paws</u>.
6. He paws are <u>soft</u>.
7. His claws are <u>sharp</u>.
8. Punch keeps <u>mice</u> away from the house.

## Page 7 More verbs

**A**
1. hiding
2. skating
3. dancing
4. writing
5. riding
6. diving
7. waving
8. driving

**B**
1. riding
2. hiding
3. waving
4. writing
5. driving
6. diving
7. dancing
8. skating

## Page 8 Statements

**A**
1. Butter is made from milk.
2. Honey is made by bees.
3. Sugar has a sweet taste.
4. The school bus was late today.
5. Mary had dinner at school.
6. I put some coal on the fire.
7. We go blackberrying in the autumn.
8. The crocus is a spring flower.
9. The elephant has a long trunk.
10. A young cat is called a kitten.

**B**
Own answers.

## Page 9 Questions

**A**

1. How are you today?
2. Why were you late this morning?
3. Where did you put the sweets?
4. When are you coming to see me?
5. Who told you that I was ill?
6. Which of these toys do you like best?
7. Will you come swimming with me?
8. Did you remember to post the letter?
9. Have you seen John?
10. Can you tell me the way?

**B**
Own answers.

## Page 10 The alphabet

**A**

1. e
2. z
3. t
4. g
5. l
6. d f
7. s
8. h
9. o s v
10. b e g

**B**

1. l m n o p
2. u v w x y
3. q r s t u v
4. a b c d e f
5. f g h i j k

## Page 11 Capital letters beginning a sentence

**A**

1. Honey is sweet.
2. The sun sets in the west.
3. Do you like nuts?
4. A rabbit has soft fur.
5. When will you be ready?
6. Keep off the grass.
7. This meat is very tender.
8. Are you going shopping?
9. Look where you are going.
10. What is the right time?

**B**
Own answers.

## Page 12 The Hall family

1. This is the Hall family.
2. There are five people in all.
3. The father is reading a book.
4. He is also eating a banana.
5. The mother is writing a letter.
6. The baby is sitting on the floor.
7. He has a ball in his hands.
8. The girl is playing with the cat.
9. The dog is asleep by the fire.
10. The boy is watching the television.

## Page 13  Verbs

**A**

| | | | | | | | |
|---|---|---|---|---|---|---|---|
| clapping | 5 | sitting | | | | | |
| batting | 6 | skipping | | | | | |
| running | 7 | chopping | | | | | |
| cutting | 8 | swimming | | | | | |

**B**

| | | | |
|---|---|---|---|
| 1 slipping | 5 rotting |
| 2 digging | 6 putting |
| 3 stopping | 7 shutting |
| 4 getting | 8 knitting |

## Page 14  Capital letters

**A**

I told Mary that I would play with her after tea.
When Emma fell down Lee helped her up.
I think David Maggs is taller than John Perry.
The names of the twins are Bela and Ramu.
I saw Sean Baker feeding his dog Sam.
We saw Daisy the cow being milked.
Kayleigh named her new pony Sunshine.
The name of our cat is Sooty.

**B**

Write a capital I in each space.

## Page 15  Names and initials

**A**
Mr. J. Cobb
Mr. H. Singh
Mr. D. R. Bond

**B**
1  Mrs. I. Bevan
2  Mrs. K. Robinson
2  Mrs. J. A. Davis

**C**
1  Miss J. Mason
2  Miss W. Leung
3  Miss A. M. Carr

**D**
1  Dr. P. Soto
2  Dr. A. J. Browne
3  Dr. M. I. Fox

## Page 16  Rhymes

**A**

| | | | | | | | | | |
|---|---|---|---|---|---|---|---|---|---|
| man | 3 | tail | 4 | seat | 5 | bear | 6 | train |
| can |   | sail |   | meat |   | pear |   | pain |
| bee |
| see |

**B**

| | | | | | | | | | |
|---|---|---|---|---|---|---|---|---|---|
| trip | 3 | mill | 5 | line | 7 | trees | 9 | hard |
| ship |   | fill |   | fine |   | bees  |   | card |
| sore | 4 | down | 6 | peel | 8 | pull | 10 | farm |
| more |   | brown |   | feel |   | full |   | harm |

## Page 17  Plurals

**A**
four shoes
five keys
two boats
six frogs
seven apples

**B**
1 hens
2 cows
3 ships
4 pens

5 ducks
6 horses
7 boats
8 socks

9 nuts
10 sweets
11 caps
12 shoes

**C**
1 chocolates
2 sisters

3 sweets
4 claws

5 comics
6 balloons

7 books

## Page 18  Busy children

1 There are five children in the picture.
2 Two of them are boys and three are girls.
3 James has made a rabbit out of clay.
4 Louise has done a drawing and is showing it to Ian.
5 There is a jar of water in front of Ian.
6 Megan is painting a picture of a house.
7 Her picture is standing on the easel.
8 Ann has a set of coloured pencils.
9 Ian and Ann are sitting opposite each other.
10 Megan is the only child standing.

## Page 19  He and she

**A**
1 father
2 aunt
3 woman
4 nephew

5 wife
6 queen
7 sister
8 girl

**B**
1 husband
2 lord
3 uncle
4 nephew

5 brother
6 prince
7 father
8 king

## Page 20  Days of the week

1 Tuesday
2 Wednesday
3 Thursday

4 Wednesday
5 Monday
6 Sunday

7 Saturday
8 Wednesday

9 Saturday
10 Friday

## Page 21 Plurals

**A**

| | | | |
|---|---|---|---|
| bushes | 6 | peaches | |
| watches | 7 | dishes | |
| coaches | 8 | churches | |
| brushes | 9 | torches | |
| boxes | 10 | matches | |

**B**

| | | | | |
|---|---|---|---|---|
| 1 | watches | 6 | coaches | |
| 2 | bushes | 7 | brushes | |
| 3 | churches | 8 | boxes | |
| 4 | dishes | 9 | peaches | |
| 5 | matches | 10 | torches | |

## Page 22 Capital letters

**A**

London is the capital of England.
Ships sail from Dover.
He was born in Oxford.
Bath is a very old city.
Jane lives in Ashton Road, Bristol.
We went by train to York.
The aeroplane landed at Heathrow.
The biggest city in Wales is Cardiff.
Many people visit Windsor Castle.
He has moved from Station Road to Oak Avenue.

**B**
Own answers.

## Page 23 To, two and too

| | | | | | | | |
|---|---|---|---|---|---|---|---|
| to | 4 | two | 7 | too; to | 9 | to; too |
| Two; two | 5 | to | 8 | two | 10 | too; to |
| too; to; to | 6 | to | | | | |

## Page 24 Children at play

David is on roller <u>skates</u>.
He is going very <u>fast</u>.
Pavana and Ann are having a <u>skipping</u> race.
Chandra and James are playing <u>marbles</u>.
James is <u>holding</u> a marble in his right hand.
Jane is on the <u>swing</u>.
The swing hangs from a <u>branch</u> of the tree.
The trunk of the tree is very <u>thick</u>.

## Page 25  Numbers

**A**
1. seventy
2. fifty
3. forty
4. sixty
5. thirty

**B**
a. forty-two
b. ninety-seven
c. seventy-eight
d. fifty-four
e. eighty-three

**C**
a. fourteen
b. eight
c. ninety-nine
d. thirteen
e. thirty
f. five
g. twenty-one
h. eleven
i. eighty-six
j. one hundred

## Page 26  Colours

**A**
1. yellow
2. green
3. black
4. red
5. brown
6. red
7. yellow
8. white
9. red
10. white

**B**
1. green
2. red
3. green
4. yellow
5. white
6. blue
7. black
8. brown
9. red
10. grey; white

**C**
1. green
2. blue
3. red
4. white

## Page 27  Plurals

**A**
1. flies
2. ponies
3. puppies
4. berries
5. daisies
6. spies
7. stories
8. fairies
9. babies
10. ladies

**B**
1. berries
2. babies
3. puppies
4. ponies
5. stories
6. spies
7. flies
8. fairies

**C**
1. cities
2. parties
3. lorries
4. hobbies
5. butterflies

## Page 28  More plurals

**A**
1. thieves
2. shelves
3. loaves
4. halves
5. calves
6. leaves
7. sheaves
8. wolves
9. wives
10. lives
11. knives

**B**

| shelves | 3 | leaves | 5 | calves | 7 | knives |
| loaves | 4 | halves | 6 | Wolves | 8 | thieves |

## Page 29  Adding -ed to verbs

**A**

| rained | 4 | waited | 7 | filled | 9 | opened |
| played | 5 | asked | 8 | picked | 10 | fetched |
| chewed | 6 | barked | | | | |

**B**

| asked | 4 | fetched | 7 | filled | 9 | chewed |
| picked | 5 | played | 8 | rained | 10 | opened |
| barked | 6 | waited | | | | |

## Page 30  Martin's toys

Martin keeps his toys in a big cupboard.
Martin likes his clockwork train best.
His mother bought it for him.
Martin can lift his tractor off the floor with his crane.
No, most of his toys are old.

## Page 31  Using is and are/Using was and were

**A**

| is | 2 | Is | 3 | is | 4 | Is |
| are | | Are | | are | | Are |

**B**

| was | 2 | was | 3 | Was | 4 | was |
| were | | were | | Were | | were |

**C**

| is; is | 3 | was; was | 4 | is; are | 5 | were; was |
| were; was | | | | | | |

## Page 32  The alphabet

**A**

bin  bucket  caravan  fork  gate  house  ladder  post
bucket  caravan  dustbin  fork  gate  house  ladder  post

**B**

| | | | | | | | | | | | | | |
|---|---|---|---|---|---|---|---|---|---|---|---|---|---|
| 1 | an | be | do | if | pan | so | | 3 | bit | job | low | one | son | two |
| 2 | add | big | car | day | end | fat | | 4 | arm | bag | eye | got | use | why |

**C**

| | | | | | | | | | |
|---|---|---|---|---|---|---|---|---|---|
| 1 | gun | 2 | zoo | 3 | cow | 4 | wet | 5 | bell |

## Page 33  Verbs – past time

**A**

| | | | | | | | | | |
|---|---|---|---|---|---|---|---|---|---|
| 1 | sneezed | 4 | fired | 7 | used | 10 | joked |
| 2 | liked | 5 | hoped | 8 | dived | 11 | baked |
| 3 | wiped | 6 | waved | 9 | saved | 12 | moved |

**B**

| | | | | | | | | | |
|---|---|---|---|---|---|---|---|---|---|
| 1 | coughed | 4 | cooked | 7 | loved | 9 | cleaned |
| 2 | arrived | 5 | waited | 8 | looked | 10 | watched |
| 3 | cheered | 6 | cycled | | | | |

## Page 34  Adding -ed to verbs

**A**

| | | | | | | | | | |
|---|---|---|---|---|---|---|---|---|---|
| 1 | pinned | 4 | slipped | 7 | wagged | 9 | hummed |
| 2 | clapped | 5 | tapped | 8 | chopped | 10 | sipped |
| 3 | stopped | 6 | hugged | | | | |

**B**

| | | | | | | | | | |
|---|---|---|---|---|---|---|---|---|---|
| 1 | slipped | 4 | stopped | 7 | pinned | 9 | clapped |
| 2 | wagged | 5 | hugged | 8 | chopped | 10 | hummed |
| 3 | sipped | 6 | tapped | | | | |

## Page 35  Jumbled sentences

1. We get wool from the sheep.
2. The girl is climbing a tree.
3. The cow is eating some grass.
4. A donkey has very long ears.
5. The horse is pulling a cart.
6. The boy is riding a bicycle.

## Page 36  Knock down the tower

1. You need <u>four sugar lumps</u>.
2. You put <u>the sugar lumps on top of each other</u>.
3. You can see <u>the food colouring going up the tower</u>.
4. Soggy means <u>wet</u>.
5. The tower <u>falls down</u>.

## Page 37 Opposites using un

**A**

| | | | | | | | |
|---|---|---|---|---|---|---|---|
| unlock | 4 | unpack | 7 | unscrew | 10 | untie |
| unpaid | 5 | unkind | 8 | unwind | 11 | unload |
| unwell | 6 | undo | 9 | unknown | 12 | unwrap |

**B**
Own answers.

**C**

| | | | | | | | |
|---|---|---|---|---|---|---|---|
| undress | 3 | unfit | 5 | unable | 7 | unwilling |
| untidy | 4 | untrue | 6 | unhappy | 8 | unsafe |

## Page 38 Opposites – change of words

| | | | | | | | |
|---|---|---|---|---|---|---|---|
| old | 4 | weak | 7 | out | 9 | shut |
| good | 5 | cold | 8 | short | 10 | tame |
| early | 6 | soft | | | | |

## Page 39 Adding -ed to verbs

**A**

| | | | | | | | |
|---|---|---|---|---|---|---|---|
| dried | 4 | tidied | 6 | buried | 8 | fried |
| carried | 5 | cried | 7 | hurried | 9 | emptied |
| copied | | | | | | |

**B**

| | | | | | | | |
|---|---|---|---|---|---|---|---|
| hurried | 4 | carried | 6 | tidied | 8 | copied |
| fried | 5 | dried | 7 | buried | 9 | paid |
| cried | | | | | | |

## Page 40 Prepositions

| | | | | | | | |
|---|---|---|---|---|---|---|---|
| off | 4 | under | 7 | in | 9 | near |
| into | 5 | across | 8 | before | 10 | behind |
| over | 6 | on | | | | |

## Page 41 Matching parts of sentences

1 The leaves were falling from the trees.
2 Tony and Sheila are brother and sister.
3 The cat lapped up all the milk in the dish.
4 Our baby likes playing with his rattle.
5 The rabbit has a short furry tail.
6 A baby sheep is called a lamb.
7 People often catch cold in very wet weather.
8 A giraffe has a very long neck.
9 The home of a horse is called a stable.
10 In summer many people go to the seaside.

## Page 42 In the woods

| | | | | | | | |
|---|---|---|---|---|---|---|---|
| 1 | true | 4 | false | 7 | false | 9 | true |
| 2 | false | 5 | false | 8 | false | 10 | false |
| 3 | true | 6 | true | | | | |

## Page 43 Conjunctions – using and

1 Our cat is white and fluffy.
2 The room was clean and tidy.
3 Grandpa sat in the armchair and fell fast asleep.
4 The day was fine and warm.
5 I gave the newsagent fifty pence and had five pence change.
6 The farmer ploughs the fields and sows the seed.
7 We went to the park and played ball.
8 The nurse took my temperature and my pulse.
9 John had his breakfast and went to school.

## Page 44 Things we eat and drink

**A**

| | | | |
|---|---|---|---|
| 1 | bananas | 5 | tea |
| 2 | chocolate | 6 | biscuits |
| 3 | sardines | 7 | jam |
| 4 | milk | 8 | bread |

**B**

| | | | |
|---|---|---|---|
| 1 | packet | 5 | bottle |
| 2 | loaf | 6 | bunch |
| 3 | pot | 7 | bar |
| 4 | cup | 8 | tin |

## Page 45 Rhymes

**A**

1 I   2 meals   3 dinner   4 No, they don't rhyme.

**B**

| **snow** bow<br>low | **flight** right<br>night | **tree** knee<br>three | **knows** grows<br>shows |

## Page 46  Using has and have

**A**

| has | 4 has | 7 have | 9 has |
| have | 5 Has | 8 Has | 10 have |
| have | 6 Have | | |

**B**
Own answers.

**C**
Own answers.

## Page 47  Words with more than one meaning

| back | 4 lean | 6 band | 8 stick |
| calf | 5 mine | 7 left | 9 suit |
| post | | | |

## Page 48  Going to school

The name of Ann's brother is John Dawes.
Yes, John and Ann go to the same school.
Ann is in Class 1.
They live quite near the school.
Before going to school every morning John takes his dog for a long walk.
His sister feeds her two rabbits.
Snowy is white; Sooty is black.
Mrs. Davies is the lollipop lady. She sees that the children cross the road safely.

## Page 49  Same sound – different meaning

| won | 3 buy | 5 made | 7 by |
| tale | 4 one | 6 tail | 8 maid |

## Page 50  People who work

**A**

| architect | 3 doctor | 5 baker | 7 miner |
| photographer | 4 farmer | 6 dentist | 8 zoo keeper |

**B**

| | | | | | | | |
|---|---|---|---|---|---|---|---|
| 1 | dentist | 4 | cashier | 7 | pilot | 9 | photographer |
| 2 | butcher | 5 | miner | 8 | baker | 10 | architect |
| 3 | doctor | 6 | zoo keeper | | | | |

## Page 51  The not words

**A**
1. doesn't
2. weren't
3. hasn't
4. isn't
5. haven't
6. wasn't
7. don't
8. aren't

**B**
1. doesn't
2. weren't
3. hasn't
4. isn't
5. Wasn't
6. don't
7. haven't
8. aren't

**C**
1. didn't
2. couldn't
3. hadn't
4. wouldn't
5. shouldn't

## Page 52  Using do and does

**A**
1. does
2. do
3. do
4. does
5. do
6. does

**B**
1. don't
2. doesn't
3. doesn't
4. don't
5. don't
6. doesn't

## Page 53  Capital letters

**A**

| | | | | | | | |
|---|---|---|---|---|---|---|---|
| 1 | London | 5 | France | 9 | April | 12 | Jones |
| 2 | Moscow | 6 | Nelson | 10 | Monday | 13 | Arthur |
| 3 | Friday | 7 | Kenya | 11 | England | 14 | July |
| 4 | Thomson | 8 | Ahmed | | | | |

**B**
1. Did you know that I was seven last Sunday?
2. Harjit and Bela live in Church Street.
3. Roy goes to Brighton every Saturday.
4. I take my dog Chum for a walk every day.
5. Jack and Jill went up the hill.
6. Farmer Grey has a cow named Daisy.
7. We shall be flying to Paris next Tuesday.
8. The Severn is the longest river in England.

## Page 54 Caterpillar

1. The word <u>chubby</u> tells us that the caterpillar is quite fat.
2. Another word for 'brief' with five letters is <u>short</u>.
3. The caterpillar makes his cocoon by <u>spinning</u>.
4. The caterpillar changes into a <u>butterfly</u>.
5. <u>Red</u> is another word for 'crimson'.

## Page 55 Joining words

**A**
birdcage; cupboard; eggcup; flowerpot; snowman; tablecloth; teapot; wallpaper

**B**
1. headache
2. windmill
3. seaside
4. dustbin
5. horseshoe
6. handbag
7. newspaper
8. bedroom
9. football
10. doorbell

## Page 56 Verbs – past time

**A**
1. drew
2. drank
3. bit
4. flew
5. come
6. wear
7. break
8. hide
9. creep
10. did
11. fall
12. gave

**B**
1. hid
2. gave
3. flew
4. bit
5. drew
6. broke
7. did
8. wore

## Page 57 Opposites – change of word

**A**
1. pretty
2. thick
3. right
4. over
5. fresh
6. give
7. up
8. top
9. clean
10. begin
11. wet
12. low

**B**
1. down
2. finish
3. dirty
4. bottom
5. wrong
6. stale
7. give
8. under
9. thin
10. ugly

## Page 58 Same sound – different meaning

1. new
2. sea
3. not
4. knew
5. our
6. see; sea
7. not; knot
8. hour

## Page 59  Collections

**A**
1. chocolates
2. people
3. flowers
4. trees
5. cards
6. tools
7. elephants
8. sheep

**B**
1. bunch
2. herd
3. pack
4. crowd
5. flock
6. clump
7. box
8. set

## Page 60  Jane's new bicycle

1. Her Uncle Bob gave Jane her new bicycle.
2. Jane was seven when she was given the new bicycle.
3. The saddle-bag is behind the seat.
4. The saddle-bag is made of plastic.
5. On the handlebars is a large, shiny bell.
6. Jane rides her bicycle every day.
7. The lane where she rides is behind her house.
8. She rides down the lane in the evening to meet her father on his way home from work.

## Page 61  Showing ownership

1. *Imran's* bat
2. *Sarah's* teddy bear
3. *Ann's* ball
4. *Oku's* top
5. *Sean's* car
6. *Jade's* pram
7. *David's* scooter
8. *Ernestine's* cat

## Page 62  Groups

**A**

**Animals**
sheep
pig
cow
goat

**Birds**
robin
thrush
rook
lark

**Trees**
beech
oak
fir
elm

**Flowers**
tulip
daisy
pansy
rose

**B**

**Tools**
spanner
hammer
axe
saw

**Clothes**
coat
shirt
shorts
jersey

**Furniture**
table
chair
settee
wardrobe

**Colours**
green
yellow
blue
brown

## Page 63  Similars

**A**
1. begin
2. crawl
3. pull
4. big
5. talk
6. stop
7. fat
8. rip
9. gift
10. end

**B**
1. large
2. speak
3. finish
4. tug
5. present
6. creep
7. halt
8. start

**C**
1. huge
2. bunch
3. show
4. valuable
5. clap

## Page 64  Adjectives

**A**
1. savage
2. shady
3. rough
4. gold
5. silk
6. blazing
7. tasty
8. fast
9. kind
10. sour

**B**
Own answers.

**C**
Own answers.

## Page 65  Same sound – different meaning

1. pair
2. sun
3. hair
4. week
5. pear
6. hare
7. weak
8. son

## Page 66  Making a snowman

1. The boys made the head of the snowman first.
2. David made a huge pile of snow for the body.
3. John and Peter put the head on the body.
4. The boys used two bits of coal for the eyes.
5. The carrot was used for the nose.
6. John stuck an old clay pipe in the snowman's mouth.
7. Peter put an old bowler hat on the snowman's head.
8. Own answer.

## Page 67   Conjunctions – using but

1. Elsa looked for her lost book but could not find it.
2. We hoped to go out but it was too wet.
3. Tim fell off his scooter but he did not hurt himself.
4. The postman rang the bell but could not get an answer.
5. They hurried to the station but the train had gone.
6. Preshani felt ill but she did not want to stay in bed.
7. Ann wanted a chocolate but the box was empty.
8. I longed for some ice-cream but I had no money.
9. We went into the park but we did not stay long.

## Page 68   Rhymes

**A**

1. night
2. alight
3. street
4. feet
5. back
6. sack
7. still
8. will

**B**
Own answers.

## Page 69   Using did and done

**A**

1. did
2. done
3. done
4. did
5. did
6. done
7. did
8. done
9. did
10. done

**B**

1. did
2. done
3. did
4. done
5. did
6. done
7. did
8. did
9. did
10. done

**C**
Own answers.

## Page 70   Putting sentences in order

1. c  e  a  d  b
2. d  b  a  e  c
3. e  a  d  c  d
4. d  c  a  e  b

## Page 71    Conjunctions – using because

**A**
1  Liam was very happy because he was on holiday.
2  He did not drink his tea because it was cold.
3  Ben was excited because he was going to Disneyland.

**B**
1  Peter dropped the cup and it broke.
2  Rajiv went into the park and had a ride on the swing.
3  Alison opened the door and crept in.

**C**
1  It was a lovely hat but it was too small for Penny.
2  We waited for Anna but she did not turn up.
3  Felix wants to buy a bicycle but he hasn't got enough money.

**D**
1  but                2  and                3  because

## Page 72    In the garden

1  Mrs. Hall cuts the grass once a week.
2  I can tell Mrs. Hall uses an electric mower because I can see the lead.
3  Penny likes digging up the weeds.
4  A pair of shears is used for trimming the hedges.
5  A vase is a container for flowers.
6  Mr. Hall has a bonfire at the bottom of the garden.
7  Mr. Hall grows potatoes, carrots, cabbages and runner beans (amongst others).
8  Philip helps by taking the weeds to the bonfire.

## Page 73    Using commas in a list

1  Robert, Andrew, Michael and Peter were ill.
2  The fishmonger had hake, plaice, herrings, mackerel and cod.
3  London, York, Birmingham and Exeter are all cities.
4  The colours of the rainbow are red, orange, yellow, green, blue, indigo and violet.
5  At the zoo we saw lions, tigers, elephants, camels and monkeys.
6  You can play rounders, netball, tennis and cricket at the holiday club.
7  Shushana's mother, brother, sister and grandfather came to the school fête.
8  The fruit bowl was piled high with apples, pears, oranges, grapes, bananas and kiwi fruit.
9  Kate put her jeans, a T-shirt and a warm sweater in her rucksack.
10  Mark carefully dried the forks, knives and spoons.

**B**
Own answers.

## Page 74 Where they live

**A**
1 web
2 stable
3 kennel
4 hive
5 burrow
6 nest

**B**
1 birds
2 rabbit or guinea pig
3 lion, tiger or fox
4 fish
5 cows

## Page 75 Adjectives

**A**
1 heavy
2 fresh
3 bright
4 china
5 sharp
6 happy
7 juicy
8 wooden

**B**
1 clean
2 ripe
3 rich
4 quiet
5 fine
6 stale
7 new
8 tidy

**C**
Own answers.

## Page 76 Hidden words

**A**
1 an
2 if
3 at
4 of
5 in
6 am
7 is
8 on
9 as
10 or

**B**
1 rat
2 oak
3 ant
4 car
5 ear
6 cow
7 arm
8 tea
9 egg
10 lip

## Page 77 Using saw and seen

**A**
1 saw
2 seen
3 saw
4 seen
5 saw
6 seen
7 saw
8 seen
9 saw
10 seen

**B**
1 seen
2 saw
3 seen
4 saw
5 saw
6 seen
7 seen
8 saw
9 seen
10 seen

## Page 78 I saw a ship a-sailing

1. The raisins were in the cabin.
2. The sails were made of satin.
3. The mast was made of gold.
4. Twenty-four sailors stood on the deck.
5. The sailors were white mice with rings about their necks.
6. The captain was a fine plump duck.
7. He had a jacket on his back.
8. The captain said Quack when the ship set sail.

## Page 79 Rhymes

**A**

1. hat, mat, cat, fat
2. lap, tap, map, rap
3. fin, win, pin, bin
4. cut, nut, but, hut
5. vest, nest, rest, west
6. dash, mash, cash, sash
7. bent, sent, lent, rent
8. seat, heat, beat, neat
9. pack, sack, rack, back

**B**

1. lame
2. name
3. game
4. flame
5. same
6. tame
7. frame
8. blame

## Page 80 Adjectives – adding -er and -est

**A**
1. taller
2. highest
3. neatest
4. warmest
5. older
6. sharper

**B**
1. finer
2. nicest
3. riper
4. tamest
5. wisest
6. paler

## Page 81 Beginning and ending sentences

**A**
Own answers.

**B**
Own answers.

## Page 82  Similars

**A**
1. wide
2. look
3. lift
4. mend
5. help
6. rich
7. right
8. answer
9. home
10. goodbye

**B**
1. hard
2. cold
3. cunning
4. small
5. smell
6. cure
7. fear
8. tiredness

## Page 83  Two word games

**A**
1. pink
2. hold
3. spin
4. learn
5. price
6. beach
7. sweep
8. beast

**B**
1. lift
2. chin
3. leaf
4. race
5. each
6. team
7. last
8. over

## Page 84  Going for a picnic

1. The Brown family went to the woods.
2. They looked for conkers.
3. She was frightened because adders can hurt you.
4. Grass snakes can't hurt you.
5. They had sausages, potato salad and cakes.
6. They had Coke to drink.
7. Own answer.

## Page 85  Things which are alike

**A**
1. ice
2. snow
3. gold
4. toast
5. rake
6. lead
7. feather
8. honey
9. mouse
10. snail

**B**
1. warm
2. sweet
3. good
4. cold
5. white
6. slow
7. light
8. thin

**C**
Own answers.

## Page 86  Adjectives – adding -er and -est

**A**
1. hottest
2. flatter
3. wettest
4. biggest
5. redder
6. saddest

**B**
1. happiest
2. lazier
3. prettier
4. tidiest
5. noisier
6. merriest
7. funnier
8. slimier
9. earlier
10. hairiest

## Page 87  Joining sentences using before

1. Jake put on thick socks before he pulled on his wellington boots.
2. Sam wrapped the present carefully before he gave it to his mother.
3. Jo carefully looked left and right before she crossed the road.
4. Kim said his prayers before he fell asleep.
5. Think carefully before you tell me the answer.

**B**
Own answers.

## Page 88  Pronouns

**A**
1. Alan told Jamie that he would help him.
2. The rabbit ran away when it heard a dog barking.
3. Anna and Talika said that they would call again.
4. Mrs. Grey has two Siamese cats. She adores them.
5. Marie promised June that she would feed the dog for her.

**B**
1. You always make me laugh.
2. David's mother said that he was feeling ill.
3. (No pronouns).
4. Mum will be cross if we don't find the key.
5. We are lost.
6. Please tell me the truth.
7. You need three fillings.
8. (No pronouns).
9. They will be here soon.
10. I lost it yesterday.
11. She is very sorry.
12. I saw you put it in the drawer.

## Page 89 Looking back

**A**
1. bottom
2. empty
3. early
4. ugly
5. right
6. wild
7. dirty
8. stale

**B**
1. leaves
2. babies
3. boxes
4. wives
5. stories
6. brushes
7. coaches
8. ladies

**C**
1. cleanest
2. biggest
3. happiest
4. ripest
5. hottest
6. longest
7. finest
8. thinnest

**D**
1. web
2. burrow
3. den
4. nest
5. aquarium
6. kennel
7. stable
8. hive

**E**
1. talk
2. wide
3. start
4. rich
5. right
6. fat
7. big
8. mend

**F**
1. maid
2. knot
3. tale
4. one
5. buy
6. sea
7. hour
8. knew

## Page 90 The summer holidays

1. Melly lives in London.
2. Becca lives next door to Melly.
3. Anna is going to France on holiday.
4. Jane is going to work in a stables.
5. Melly is going to stay with her grandmother.
6. There are two weeks in a fortnight.
7. Own answer giving reasons.